DATE			

ORLANDO GIBBONS
and his family

Orlando Gibbons

ORLANDO GIBBONS

and his family

{3C3}

THE LAST OF THE
TUDOR SCHOOL OF MUSICIANS

{3C3}

EDMUND H. FELLOWES

C.H., M.V.O., M.A.
Mus.D., Oxford, Cambridge, and Dublin
Hon. Fellow of Oriel College, Oxford

SECOND EDITION

ARCHON BOOKS
1970

Reprinted 1970 with permission
Oxford University Press
in an unaltered and unabridged edition

FIRST PUBLISHED 1925
SECOND EDITION 1951

SBN: 208 00848 9
LIBRARY OF CONGRESS CATALOG CARD NUMBER: 79-95024
[REPRODUCED FROM A COPY IN THE YALE UNIVERSITY LIBRARY]
PRINTED IN THE UNITED STATES OF AMERICA

PREFACE
TO THE SECOND EDITION

WHEN this short book was first printed, the name of Orlando Gibbons was little known outside a small circle of specialists. Nevertheless, he was not entirely forgotten, as were most of the great choral composers of the Tudor School, both of sacred and secular music; 'Hosanna' and 'Almighty and Everlasting God' were in general use in most English cathedrals, having retained their position as popular favourites during the three centuries of their existence. Gibbons's lovely madrigal 'The Silver Swan' also remained a favourite wherever madrigals continued to be sung. In this respect he enjoyed a popularity that was denied to almost all his great colleagues. But it was small. Indeed, it remains sadly true that twenty-five years ago this great English composer was practically unknown to his countrymen.

Times have changed. Gibbons's book of twenty-one madrigals is published complete as volume v in *The English School of Madrigal Composers*. His Church music is collected and issued as volume iv of *Tudor Church Music*. Much of his instrumental music, both for strings in consort and for keyboard, is available in print in practical editions; the madrigals and a large part of the Church music are also published in separate numbers.

It is fitting that a new edition of this book should be issued, with so much more material available for study and performance; but also because modern research has revealed much that is new concerning the personal history of this great English musician and his family.

The author's thanks are especially due to Mrs. F. A. Keynes of Cambridge, and Mr. G. A. Thewlis of Oxford, who independently drew his attention to the Records of the City of Oxford, as edited by Mr. H. E. Salter, and other documents, by which it is plainly proved that Orlando Gibbons, as suspected by the author in the former edition, was born in Oxford, and not in Cambridge as stated on his monument in Canterbury Cathedral.

1951   E. H. F.

PREFACE
TO THE FIRST EDITION

ALTHOUGH born forty years later than William Byrd, Orlando Gibbons survived him by less than two years, and the celebration of the three-hundredth anniversary of Byrd's death in 1923 is followed in the present year by that of Gibbons. The need for a short book giving some account of his life and work is therefore very similar to that which was felt in regard to Byrd two years ago, and although the interest in the work of the Elizabethan composers has shown immense development during that time, yet there are still many people who know little or nothing of Gibbons. Beyond the articles in Grove's *Dictionary of Music and Musicians*, the *Dictionary of National Biography*, and the histories of Walker and Davey, Orsmond Anderton's *Early English Music*, Bridge's *Twelve Good Musicians*, and the present writer's *English Madrigal Composers* there is not much printed information about this composer, and much that has been printed needs revision and correction in the light of modern research. Few people, even in cathedral circles, until lately could have named more than about half a dozen works by Gibbons, at a liberal estimate; yet it is true that his name has been kept alive more successfully than that of any of the Tudor composers except perhaps Tallis. For some reason his service in F survived in continuous use at almost every cathedral in England even though Byrd's short service was neglected in many of these establishments. 'Hosanna' has been kept alive in almost every cathedral and so has the beautiful little Collect 'Almighty and everlasting God'. In secular surroundings 'The silver swan' has been a favourite wherever madrigals have been sung. But outside these four works hardly a note of Gibbons's music was known until recently except in very circumscribed surroundings. Yet more than 150 of his compositions are known to exist to-day, and a very large proportion of these have been published in modern editions. Gibbons has, however, survived as at least a living name, even when his greater contemporary Byrd was forgotten. Yet it cannot be contended that even now he takes the place that he deserves in the estimation of most English people, and it is to be hoped that this small book may serve the purpose of introducing many to this outstanding figure in English music.

The author desires to express his gratitude to the Trustees of the Carnegie United Kingdom Trust for permission to use the material which he compiled for the Preface of vol. iv of the Carnegie edition of *Tudor Church Music*. He also acknowledges his indebtedness to many friends who have assisted him in various ways; among these he would mention Mr. Arthur Cochrane, *Chester Herald*, Rev. R. C. B. Llewellyn,

Succentor and Custos of the College of Vicars Choral of Exeter Cathedral, Rev. Canon A. J. Mason, D.D., and Dr. Charlton Palmer of Canterbury Cathedral, Rev. Chancellor Wordsworth of Salisbury Cathedral, Mr. Boris Ord of King's College, Cambridge, Mr. Noel Ponsonby of Ely Cathedral, and his three colleagues on the Editorial Committee of the Carnegie edition of *Tudor Church Music*, Dr. Percy Buck, Rev. A. Ramsbotham, and Miss Townsend Warner. To Miss Margaret H. Glyn he is especially indebted for permission to quote from her book *All about Elizabethan Virginal Music*, and more particularly for the detailed list of Gibbons's keyboard music printed in that book with references as to source of text, together with some additional details with which she kindly supplied him.

1925   E. H. F.

CONTENTS

ILLUSTRATIONS

CHAPTER I
A Family of Musicians[1]

WILLIAM, EDWARD, ELLIS, AND FERDINANDO

ORLANDO GIBBONS had the advantage of being born into a musical family, and musical surroundings. William Boyce somewhat loosely translated the Latin phrase on his monument in Canterbury Cathedral as a statement that he was 'born among the Muses and Musick'.[1] But the statement is a true one, because his father and three of his brothers, two of whom were several years older than he, were musicians; and, as a consequence his gifts were recognized and nurtured from his earliest existence. Cambridge, his home from early childhood, was a musical centre then as now, so that before he became a chorister at King's College he must have become familiar with most of the master-pieces of Elizabethan Church music which were being performed daily in the famous college choirs at Cambridge.

Yet, as we shall see, he was an Oxford boy.

[1] Boyce, *Cathedral Music*, vol. i, p. viii, and Dart, *History and Antiquitie. of Canterbury*, pp. 51–2.

WILLIAM GIBBONS

Orlando was the tenth and youngest child of William Gibbons, a musician of considerable gifts, and of Mary his wife, whose maiden name is not known though it may have been Ellis. In the light of recent research among the Oxford City Records, as far as the few facts about William Gibbons are known, his story needs to be restated.

There is good evidence to show that this William was a son of Richard Gibbons, a prominent Oxford citizen; and that he was born at Oxford. Richard occupied himself for many years with municipal affairs. He is first heard of in 1550 when he was admitted as a 'Hanaster' or Councillor of the City of Oxford.[1] In 1562 he was suspended from office 'for insulting conduct', probably not of a serious nature, because he was readmitted very shortly afterwards. He was one of the two city chamberlains in 1569. His name still appears on the list of hanasters in 1583, the year in which his son William was admitted to this same office. Further evidence that William was his son is supplied by the fact that exceptionally small fees were charged on his admission as a hanaster, for it was customary to accept a generous reduction in the case of father and son.

Nothing more is known of Richard. He was probably born about 1515.

[1] *Oxford City Properties*, ed. H. E. Salter, 1926.

It is worth mentioning here that in 1435 a John Gebons, living in Oxford, was summoned among the jury at the Exchequer, to decide whether members of the University had been duly assessed for the subsidy by Thomas Chace, late Chancellor.

It is probable that William Gibbons was born in Oxford about the years 1540–2, and that his youth was spent there. It is known that he had come to live in Cambridge at least as early as 1566, because in that year his eldest son Richard (note the name) was baptized at Holy Trinity Church. The date and details of his marriage have not been found. Possibly it was his marriage that brought him to Cambridge. But more likely it was to take up appointment as a lay clerk at King's or some other college, because, like his sons, he also was a trained musician. He remained in Cambridge until about 1579 or 1580, during which time seven or eight of his children were born and baptized in Holy Trinity Church.

Soon after his arrival in Cambridge, 'in the tenth year of our sovereign ladie Quene Elizabeth (1567)' William Gibbons was admitted one of the 'waytes' of the city, when 'Mr. Maior did delyver to William Gibons musician fyve sylver collers called the waites collers, pondering xxij oz. i d. And the said William Gibbons hathe found sureties for the delyverye of the same Collers agayne when they be required'.[1]

[1] Corporation Common Day Book, 1567, 25th November.

The appointment is in itself evidence of high musical skill. At that period the waits constituted an important feature in civic life. They were small bands of competent musicians maintained at the expense of the civic authorities, and their principal duty was to perform at municipal functions. All the larger cities in England at that time were provided with such bands and their proficiency may be judged from the high praise bestowed upon them by William Kempe, the famous Elizabethan comedian and dancer. Writing of the Norwich Waits in 1599 Kempe noted 'their excellency in wind instruments, their rare cunning on the Vyoll and Violin, theyr voices be admirable, everie one of them able to serve in any Cathedral Church in Christendoome for Quiristers'.[1] In comparing the conditions of life in Elizabethan England with those of today, musicians may reasonably deplore the disestablishment of these municipally supported bands of skilled musicians.

Various other documents connect William with Cambridge during this period, giving evidence that he was living there in fairly affluent circumstances. On the 31st July 1573 'William Gibbons of Cambridge, musician, in consideration of £30, sold to John Hatcher of Cambridge, M.D., a messuage in the parish of St. Edward's, adjoining another tenement of William Gibbons, then lately belonging to Corpus Christi College'.[2]

[1] Kempe, *Nine daies Wonder* reprinted in *Collectanea Adamantae*, No. 24.
[2] C. H. Camden, *Annals of the University and Town of Cambridge*, p. 176 n.

On the 11th August 1573 Mary, the wife of William Gibbons, released to Dr. Hatcher her dower in the premises.[1] In 1574, and again in 1578, William signed the vestry book at Holy Trinity Church. On the 1st June 1578 the proctors complained to the Vice-Chancellor that William Gibbons[2] 'did upholde, maintain and kepe or cause to be kept a dansing schole within the Town of Cambridge, and Gibbons confessing the same' was fined 40s. In 1579 William resigned his membership of the city waits and was succeeded by one John Martin. This step seems to have been taken in anticipation of his impending return to Oxford.

Although it is probable that he was back in Oxford at least as early as 1581 no actual mention of him has been found before 1583, in which year he was made a city councillor, or hanaster. But it is unlikely that he would have been appointed immediately on his return. On the 21st December 1583[3] land in the Priory and Fair of the Augustine Friars, now the site of Wadham College, was occupied by William Gybbons and others for a lease of twenty-one years at a rental of £10. In 1586 it was still in their possession when it was sold to the city of Oxford by William Frere.[4] On Christmas Day 1583 the baptism of William's famous son,

---

[1] Op. cit. Bowtell MSS., Downing College, Edward Hall's Register.

[2] Cooper, *Annals of Cambridge*, vol. v, p. 305.

[3] *City of Oxford Records*, ed. W. H. Turner.

[4] *Oxford City Properties*, ed. H. E. Salter, 1926.

Orlando, was recorded in the register of St. Martin's Church, now incorporated with All Saints' in the city of Oxford.

It was on the 15th September 1588 that, as the city records show, William Gibbons delivered up to one George Bucknall the badges of the waits of which body he had evidently become a member at Oxford, as he had been at Cambridge. He then returned to Cambridge for the rest of his life.

The earliest record of the name of Gibbons at King's College is in the 'Mundum' or Bursar's books of accounts in 1590. At this date and from time to time, small payments were made to 'Mr. Gibbons' for musical performances on festive occasions. The earlier entries may refer to William Gibbons, but thenceforward the name appears as Edward Gibbons.

William died at Cambridge and was buried at Holy Trinity on the 20th October 1595. His nuncupative will[1] was dated in the month of October 1595; it was proved on the 13th November following, in the Cambridge Archidiaconal Court by his widow Marie Gibbon, to whom he bequeathed 'all his goods whatsoever to dispose amongest his children as she should thinck convenient and at her discretion'. The witnesses were 'Humfrye Tredwaye M^r of Arts' and 'Edward Gibbon Batchelour of Musicke'.

[1] Cambs. Arch. Court, vol. v, f. 183, at the Peterborough Registry, *and see* Appendix.

Details of William Gibbons's marriage are not known; but if Richard, buried at Great St. Mary's in July 1566, was the eldest child and died in infancy, as seems likely, the date of marriage may be put at about 1565. The widow died at Cambridge in April 1603 and was buried at Holy Trinity on the 19th of that month. Her will was dated the 17th March 1602/3, with a codicil dated the 11th April 1603, the witnesses being James 'Deyer', her son-in-law, and Orlando Gibbons. It was proved by her son and sole executor, Ellis Gibbons, in the Cambridge Archidiaconal Court[1] on the 21st April 1603. She left legacies to her daughters, Elizabeth Dyer and Jane Gibbons; to each of her sons, Ferdinando and Orlando, £26. 13s. 4d. to be paid them respectively when they should reach the ages of twenty-three and twenty-one. It may be observed that Orlando was nineteen years old at this date. The other daughters, Thomasine Hopper and Mary, wife of Christopher Edmondes, are also mentioned. Edward, the eldest surviving son, had no legacy except 'for himself and his wief each of them a mourning gowne', but his two children Mary and Joan were given 'my silver beaker' and 'the little guilte cupp'. Ellis, besides being executor, was also residuary legatee, his mother being 'fullie resolved of his zeale to god and dutifull affection to me'. His wife Joan was also left a mourning gown. Ellis survived his mother by less than a month.

[1] Cambs. Arch. Court, vol. vi, f. 152.

Of the sons Edward, Ellis, Ferdinando, and Orlando, more in detail presently. Of the daughters, Thomasine seems to have been the eldest; she married Thomas Hopper on the 1st May 1598 at Holy Trinity, Cambridge. Two of her children, Mary and Agnes, were baptized at Holy Trinity on the 25th March 1598/9 and the 22nd December 1600 respectively. Elizabeth married James Dyer, or Dier, at Holy Trinity on the 13th November 1600; Ann, their daughter, was baptized at Holy Trinity on the 22nd November 1601; she inherited £20 under the will of her uncle, Ellis Gibbons, in 1603. Elizabeth and her husband were witnesses of Ellis's will.[1] Mary is the first of the daughters whose baptism was registered at Holy Trinity; the date is the 27th February 1578/9. She married Christopher Edmondes before the year 1602, as we learn from her mother's will. Jane, the youngest daughter, was baptized at Holy Trinity on the 5th April 1580. She was unmarried at the date of her mother's death. Susan, another daughter, was buried at Great St. Mary's in 1576, but there is no clue to her age.

EDWARD GIBBONS

Edward the eldest surviving son was baptized at Great St. Mary's, Cambridge, on the 21st March 1567/8. He graduated B.Mus. at Cambridge and was incorporated in the same degree at Oxford on the 7th

[1] P.C.C. 32 Bolein.

July 1592.[1] The earliest record connecting him with King's College is in the 'Liber Communarum'. In Annunciation Term 1592/3 he was receiving a salary of 20s. a quarter as a lay-clerk. At that date Thomas Hammond was Informator or Master of the Choristers and continued in that office until the following Michaelmas Term, when Edward Gibbons took his place, with a quarterly addition of 11s. 8d. to his salary. The office of organist is never mentioned in the college records in connexion with either Hammond or Gibbons. Gibbons was Master of the Choristers until the autumn of 1598 when Hammond resumed the position, and the name of Edward Gibbons disappears from the books. Meanwhile in 1595 he figured as witness of his father's will, and it is possible that he succeeded his father as a member of the Cambridge Waits, for in the Bursar's books at Jesus College there is record of payment 'to Gibbons the musition 6s. 8d.' for performing with the waits in the college hall at a feast in the year 1596/7, and this must refer to Edward. Exactly what became of him between 1598 and 1607 when he was settled at Exeter is not known, but he seems to have left Cambridge in 1598. The only certain fact about him is that in 1603 he was described in the will of his brother Ellis[2] as 'of Acton'. Presumably this was the village of Acton in Middlesex, but no record has been discovered to

---

[1] Foster's *Alumni Oxon.* sub Edward Gibbons. Wood's *Fasti Oxon.*, ed. Bliss, vol. i. 258. [2] P.C.C. 32 Bolein.

throw any light upon what he was doing there, and possibly the phrase only meant that he owned property there. It has been generally stated by historians, following Anthony Wood, that he became Organist and Precentor of Bristol Cathedral, also that he was in Holy Orders. Walker, Boyce, Hawkins, and Burney are among those who repeated these statements, and they find a place in the *Dictionary of National Biography*. Nevertheless, recent research proves clearly that he remained a layman to the end of his life; the Bristol Cathedral records, covering these years with complete detail, have lately been brought to light but make no mention of the name in connexion with any office. It is not impossible that he may have been organist of one of the city churches in Bristol, for the tradition is of early origin.

Dr. John Walker,[1] writing in 1714, says that he was brought to Exeter by Dr. Cotton when the latter was preferred to the see of Exeter. And it would seem that he was already working at the cathedral in some unofficial capacity earlier than 1607, for on the 24th October that year the baptism of William, son of Edward Gibbons, is recorded in the cathedral registers. William Cotton became Bishop of Exeter in November 1598; and if Walker is right, it is quite likely that Cotton brought Edward Gibbons to Exeter in 1598; for the date happens to coincide with his disappearance from King's and this

---

[1] Walker's *An Attempt towards recovering an Account of the Numbers and Sufferings of the Clergy*, &c., pt. ii, p. 32.

would provide a consecutive account of his life. On the 25th March 1609 the Exeter Chapter[1] 'decreed a patente to be made to Mr Gibbons Bachelor of Musicke of xx^{li} per annum so longe to continue as he shall teache the choristers and secondaries of this churche in instrumentall musicke'. This minute, with its reference to instrumental music, is in itself of great interest; and it must be explained that the term 'secondaries' refers to supernumerary musicians who unlike the 'lay vicars' were not members of the foundation. It is possible that for some years, or ever since 1598, he was engaged on teaching instrumental music to members of the choir before he became officially connected with the cathedral. The Chapter then nominated Gibbons 'to a Vicar's place now void by the departure of George Tucker . . . so as the said Gibbins by reason of his degree in musicke or dispensac̄on from my Lo. Bishoppe of Exon to whome the disposing thereof is come by lapse the same shall be approved and consented to'. This curious minute implies some irregularity of sufficient importance to call for episcopal dispensation; and the explanation is, no doubt, that Gibbons was a layman. He was also the protégé of Bishop Cotton, as Walker stated, and in appointing Gibbons the Dean and Chapter may have been acting under pressure from Bishop Cotton who, it may be recalled, was notorious for his conduct in the exercise of preferment for his friends and relatives.

[1] Exeter Cath. Chapter Act Book, No. 3553, ff. 11-12.

Dispensation was duly granted, and on the 8th August 1609[1] he was admitted a priest vicar. Having taken the oath, he was assigned a 'place and stall in the choir, vacant by the cession and deprivation of George Tucker'.

The College of Vicars Choral of Exeter kept independent records apart from those of the Chapter. The original documents of the vicars were lost at an early date, but an early eighteenth-century extract from the 'Antient Account bookes' survives in the charge of the present Custos of the college. These books show 'a chasme in time' between 1607 and 1628. In this latter year Gibbons was one of the four priest vicars and in that year he was also Custos of the college. The Custos was, and still is, elected annually from among the priest vicars by all the members of the college including the lay vicars. In accordance with prevailing practice Gibbons held this office only from time to time, and not permanently as has usually been implied. The Cathedral Registers show that in 1627 Thomas Irishe was Custos; in 1634 Thomas Gales held the same office,[2] and at Michaelmas 1645 when Gibbons's name appears in the books of the vicars choral for the last time, another of the priest vicars was Custos. After 1645 there is another 'chasme till ye yeare 1660' so that there is no record in these books to show when Edward Gib-

---

[1] Exeter Cath. Chapter Act Book, No. 3553, f. 14.
[2] *Hist. MSS. Comm. Report*, iv, App. 137.

bons died. Meanwhile it is recorded[1] that on the 29th January 1615 Archbishop Abbot issued a mandate to the Dean and Chapter of Exeter to appoint 'Master Edward Gibbons Mus Bac, Custos of the College of Vicars Chorel' to be Succentor. Consequently on the 15th February the Chapter[2] decreed that he should be installed in that office. This appointment may perhaps explain the tradition that he was organist of the cathedral, for there was no provision for an organist on the foundation, and the succentor was probably responsible for the duty of organ-playing either in person or by deputy.

But Gibbons exposed himself to a charge of serious neglect of his duties in the choir, and moreover, owing to the fact that he was not in Holy Orders, his colleagues were dissatisfied with his appointment, notwithstanding the bishop's dispensation. Other instances are on record of a layman becoming a priest vicar or minor canon in cathedral establishments in the seventeenth and eighteenth centuries, but the case of Gibbons became the subject of formal protest on the part of two of the lay vicars in 1634, who at Laud's visitation[3] complained not only that there were four instead of six priest vicars, but that 'one of them was a leaman namely Mr Edward Gibbins. . . . The fore named Mr Edward

---

[1] Lambeth Register of Archbishop Abbot, vol. i, f. 415 rev.

[2] Exeter Cath. Chapter Acts, No. 3554, ff. 11–12.

[3] *Hist. MSS. Comm. Report*, iv, App. 137.

Gibbins doth not sitt in his place and read and singe at devine service tyme as the rest doth but once a quarter or ther about doth sitt in his place for two or three dayes but doth not usially do it as yᵉ rest.' The 'Answeare of the Custos and coll: of yᵉ Vicars Coralls' was signed by 'Thomas Gales Costos, Edward Gibbins, John Mayne and John Frost'.[1]

Walker's account has already been mentioned.[2] It has some value in that it was written scarcely more than half a century after his death. He says that Gibbons

'married two wives which were Gentlewomen of Considerable Families and Fortunes; the first a near relation of the Lord Spencer's, and the second of the ancient family of the Bluets in this County, By which means he had gotten a very considerable temporal estate, insomuch that I have been informed by an ancient Gentleman who was related to him he presented his Majesty when under his distresses to the value of a Thousand Pound. When the Rebellion was prevalent in this County and the Parliamentary Commissioners were raising contributions here, they demanded of him £500, and upon his refusing to pay it they plundered his house . . . and turned him and his wife (both then aged between 80 and 90) and three grandchildren out of doors. . . . He built two little Oratories on two estates which he had in this County, one of which at least within the Parish of Dunsford is remaining to this day.'

That Gibbons was wealthy seems true, for on the 25th January 1636/7 he was taxed for ship money, 'Over

[1] *Hist. MSS. Comm. Report*, iv, p. 139.

[2] Walker's *An Attempt towards recovering an Account of the Numbers and Sufferings of the Clergy*, &c., pt. ii, p. 32.

and above 13*s*. 4*d*. as a priest vicar of the cathedral is taxed, at £1. 6*s*. 8*d*. for his temporal estate'.[1]

Edward Gibbons married his first wife, said by Walker to be a relative of Lord Spencer, before 1597; for in that year his son Robert was baptized on the 1st July and buried on the 5th July at Holy Trinity, Cambridge. She was mentioned in the will of Edward's mother, who, as already stated, left pieces of plate to his daughters Mary and Joan. Mary was baptized at Holy Trinity on the 11th April 1599 and is perhaps to be identified with Mary Gibbons who on the 4th May 1628 married Greenwood Randall at Exeter Cathedral. On the same day at the cathedral Jane Gibbons married Thomas Gale and she may also have been a daughter of Edward. Joan, who inherited her grandmother's 'guilte cupp', is without doubt to be identified with the Joan, daughter of Edward, who was buried at Exeter Cathedral on the 19th June 1627. William Gibbons, son of Edward, as already mentioned, was baptized at Exeter Cathedral on the 24th October 1607. On the 28th February 1636 Murry, or Murray, Gibbons, son of Edward, was buried at the cathedral; he had a son Edward who died young, and his widow Mary married secondly James Lake. It is not unlikely that Major Robert Gibbons who became Governor of the Castle of Exeter on the 17th June 1647[2] was another son.

[1] *Domestic State Papers, Charles I*, vol. cccxliv, No. 102.
[2] Ibid., vol. dxv, No. 82.

Edward's first wife Jane was buried at Exeter Cathedral on the 7th April 1628, for the entry in the burial register of the cathedral on the 9th January 1664 no doubt refers to his widow. The name of Gibbons seems to have developed strongly in and around Exeter in the eighteenth century and may represent the descendants of Edward Gibbons. It is probable that Edward died before 1650, but the precise date is not known. An exhaustive search for his will at Exeter and Somerset House has proved abortive.

Little evidence of Edward's work as a composer has survived. In Tudway's collection in the British Museum[1] is 'A prelude upon yᵉ Organ as was then usuall before yᵉ Anthem by Mʳ Edward Gibbons, Custos of yᵉ College of Preist-vicars of Exeter 1611'. Also the anthem 'How hath the city sate solitary'. At Christ Church, Oxford, is a three-voice anthem 'Awake and arise' and a setting of the Kyrie and Creed to go with William Mundy's short service. In the Bodleian Library is an *In Nomine* of five parts.[2] The statement that there are compositions of his among the manuscripts of the Royal College of Music is incorrect.

ELLIS GIBBONS

Ellis, the third son of William and Mary Gibbons, was baptized at Holy Trinity, Cambridge, on the 30th

[1] Harl. MS. 7340, f. 193ᵇ.
[2] Bodl. MS. Mus. Sch. D, 412–16.

November 1573. The statement that he became organist of Salisbury Cathedral has been reiterated by many musical historians, but it seems to be entirely void of foundation. No trace of his name can be found at Salisbury either in the cathedral or elsewhere. There is a gap in the Chapter Act Books between the book 'Penruddock', which ends on the 9th September 1597, and 'Mortimer', which begins on the 12th August 1603. But the 'Clerk of Fabrik' accounts cover this period with full details and show that Richard Fuller received payment 'for the orgenes' from Lady Day 1592 to Michaelmas 1598, at which date John Farrant succeeded him, and that John Holmes succeeded Farrant in 1602.

Ellis Gibbons, as previously mentioned, was executor and residuary legatee of his mother's will in April 1603 and in that will his wife's name Joan is mentioned. His own will[1] fixes the date of his death almost to a day; it was executed on the 14th May 1603 and proved only four days later, and the natural inference is that he died on the 14th May. The will gives some further details which have been hitherto unknown: that he was married and left a widow but no surviving children: that his brother Edward was his executor and was then living at Acton: that he owned property in Cambridge and St. Paul's churchyard, the life-interest of which he bequeathed to his widow with remainder to his brother

[1] P.C.C. 32 Bolein, and see Appendix.

Edward. His sister, Elizabeth Dyer, and her husband were among the witnesses to the will and he gave a legacy of £20 to their child. In the printed Index of P.C.C. Wills[1] Ellis Gibbons is described as of the parish of St. Benet, Paul's Wharf. This detail is not mentioned anywhere in the will, nor is the source of the information disclosed in the printed Index; but if it be true it is consistent with the evidence that he was not at Salisbury; it is possible he was buried at St. Benet's, but the parish registers of that date have unfortunately perished and the conjecture remains entirely unsupported.

Ellis Gibbons died before he was thirty. Thomas Morley honoured him by including two of his madrigals in *The Triumphes of Oriana*, a distinction which the editor, alone among the contributors, shared with him. Of these two 'Round about her charret' is much the finer; the scoring is interesting and varied in colour and not unlike that of Orlando; and the concluding passage with its characteristic cadence, even though allowance be made for what amounted almost to a formula at this period, shows the hand of an artist. It is a strange fact that no other compositions by Ellis Gibbons have survived, whether sacred, secular, or instrumental, nor is he known to have held any musical appointment. Is it possible that these two madrigals were in reality the early work of Orlando, his junior by ten years, and

---

[1] Compiled by Dr. S. A. Smith, ed. by E. A. Fry for the British Record Society.

scarcely more than a youth when Morley was collecting the material for *The Triumphes*? The author is aware that in hazarding this suggestion he has no valid evidence to support it, but it may be worth considering.

FERDINANDO GIBBONS

Of Ferdinando, the fourth son, very little is known except for the fact that he was a musician. He was about two years older than Orlando; but details of his baptism have not as yet been discovered either at Cambridge or Oxford. It would seem that he was born shortly after the return of his father to Oxford. He is mentioned in the wills of his mother and of his brother Ellis. The fact that his mother's legacy was withheld till he was twenty-three and that Orlando was at that moment aged nineteen, point to his being born in 1581.

Ferdinando was appointed one of the city waits at Lincoln on the 8th June 1611.

CHAPTER II

A Family of Musicians—II

ORLANDO AND CHRISTOPHER

THE belief that Orlando was born in Cambridge was firmly held without question ever since the days of his life down to the present time. It was accepted as a fact by his contemporaries, and it was recorded on the monument set up in his memory in Canterbury Cathedral shortly after his death. It may even be that Orlando himself regarded Cambridge as his birthplace, for he left Oxford when still no more than four years of age, and he could have had but small recollection of his earliest home-life, especially as his numerous elder brothers and sisters were natives of Cambridge. The statement on the Canterbury monument that he was brought up in musical surroundings among musicians remains true.

Long ago Anthony Wood was puzzled by the discovery that the baptism of an Orlando Gibbons was recorded in an Oxford church in 1583. He felt doubt as to whether this entry could actually refer to the composer. Doubt about the Cambridge tradition was first expressed in modern times by the present author in a former edition of the present book, and also in the Preface to Volume IV of *Tudor Church Music*. Both of these were published in 1927. It seemed at the time a daring challenge in the face of the contemporary Canterbury statement and the unbroken tradition at King's and elsewhere. Nevertheless it is now proved beyond all possible dispute that this famous English musician was born in Oxford, where his parents were living at the time; and the mystery created by the discovery of his baptism at St. Martin's Church, Oxford, on Christmas Day 1583, is solved.

Although for at least two generations in the sixteenth century, and one earlier instance has been quoted, a branch of the Gibbons family was connected with the county of Oxford, the main stock was of East Anglian origin, especially in the neighbourhood of Lynn in Norfolk. The name is found there for many generations deriving its pedigree from one John Guybon or Gibbon, and Margaret his wife, who were living in North Lynn in the reign of Edward II. Variants of this surname, as used by known members of the family, were Guibon, Gebon, Gybon, and Gibbon; and no doubt Guybon was pronounced Gēbon. One of this family was Thomas Gibbon, Mayor of Lynn 1503–9 and High Sheriff in 1513. Robert Gibbon of South Lynn had his lands confiscated in 19 Edw. IV. The will of John Gebon of Reche, co. Camb., was proved in 1512; among his grandchildren were Thomas, Richard, and William. Gregory Guybon married an Ely lady and had a son, Thomas, who married four times and is probably to be identified with the Mayor of Lynn just mentioned. This family bore as arms: or, a lion rampant, sable, over all a bend gules, charged with three escallops, argent; this coat was recorded in the heralds' visitation. The coat is identical with that placed over the monument to Orlando Gibbons in Canterbury Cathedral. Nothing is more likely than that William, father of Orlando, belonged to some cadet branch of the Lynn family and was well aware of his claim to the coat of arms.

The sister universities share the honour of nurturing this great musician in his early infancy, just as they shared the privilege in later life of bestowing on him academic honours, Cambridge with the B.Mus., and Oxford with the D.Mus. He is recorded in the Oxford University Registers as having been incorporated on 14th July 1607 as M.A., of Cambridge. This entry puzzled Wood; but Joseph Foster suggested that M.A. was a clerical error for B.Mus. The dates fit perfectly, for he took the B.Mus. degree in 1606. The error is worth mentioning for it is unfortunately enlarged upon in *The Dictionary of National Biography*.

About 14th February 1595/6, as recorded in the 'Liber Communarum', Gibbons entered the choir of King's College, Cambridge, as a chorister. He was just twelve at the time. His brother had for three years been

a member of the choir and was at that time Master of
the Choristers. There is no evidence that Orlando was
ever senior chorister. His regular service in the choir
ceased during Michaelmas Term 1598, but his name
appears intermittently as a chorister until the second
week in May 1599. He matriculated in Easter Term
1598 as 'a sizar from King's'.[1] In the years 1602 and
1603 the 'Mundum Books' show that 'Mr Gibbons'
was paid special fees by the college, at one time 2s. 6d.,
at another 2s., 'pro musica' 'in festo Dominae Reginae',
and for the Feast of the Purification.[2] These fees were
precisely similar in amount as those paid from time to
time to his brother and were not made for music composed, as has been commonly stated, but for providing
musical performances on festive occasions.

On the 21st March 1604/5 Orlando was appointed
organist of the Chapel Royal. The appointment is recorded as follows in the Cheque Book:[3] 'Arthur Cock
died the 26th of Januarie and Orlando Gibbons sworne
in his roome the 21st, of Marche followinge.' No doubt
his brilliant gifts as an executant had already been developed, but his appointment to this leading position
at the age of twenty-one is almost more remarkable
than that of Byrd to Lincoln Cathedral at the age of
nineteen. Gibbons retained this post until the end of

---

[1] Venn's *Book of Matriculations* and *Alumni Cantabrigienses*.
[2] King's College *Mundum Books*, vol. xxi.
[3] *The Old Cheque Book of the Chapel Royal*, ed. Rimbault, p. 6.

his life. When he took the degree of B.Mus. at Cambridge in 1606, the terms of the grace were as follows:[1] 'Conceditur Orland. Gibbons regio organistae ut studium septem annorum in musica sufficiat ei ad intrandum in eadem. Sic tamen ut canticum conponat cantand. coram universitate in die comitiorum, et ut presentetur per magistrum regen. in habitu baccalaurei in artibus.'

About the year 1606 Gibbons married Elizabeth, daughter of John Patten. It is possible that she is to be identified with Elizabeth, daughter of John Patten, who was baptized at St. Margaret's, Westminster, on the 1st November 1590. Patten was at one time a Yeoman of the Vestry of the Chapel Royal.[2] In 1607 he was Keeper of the King's Closet and on the 14th November of that year[3] he received a gift of £200 from the Crown, being a fine lately imposed on Nicholas Fuller by the Commissioners for Causes Ecclesiastical. Patten died in 1623. In his will,[4] dated the 20th February 1622, he appointed his son-in-law Orlando Gibbons sole executor and residuary legatee and left £200 to Orlando's children. Among the witnesses to Patten's will was Peregrine Tomkins, brother of Thomas Tomkins.

At about this same period it is recorded in the Overseers' Books of St. Margaret's, Westminster, that

[1] Baker, *Reg. Acad. Cantab.*, quoted by Wood, *Fasti Oxonienses*, ed. Bliss, vol. i, p. 407.
[2] *The Old Cheque Book of the Chapel Royal*, ed. Rimbault.
[3] *Domestic State Papers, James I*, vol. xxviii, p. 382.
[4] P.C.C. 91 Swann.

Gibbons was living in the Woolstaple where Bridge Street now stands.[1] By this time he had earned a great reputation not only as a composer but also as the best organist in England, and it is not surprising that he should have been the recipient of royal favours. In 1611 he presented a petition to Lord Salisbury[2] as Lord High Treasurer 'shewing that the Petitioner hath bene an humble Sutor to the Queenes Matie for her gracious furtherance in procuring for him from his Highness a lease in Revertion of 40 Mark a yeare of the Duchy lands without fine . . . forasmuch as the Petitioner hath long depended upon this Sute in regard of her Maties, gracious promises to him and by reason hereof hath neglected all other oportunities of benefitt by her Highnes favor'.

On the 19th July 1615[3] Lawrence Brewster of the city of Gloucester, Gentleman, having forfeited to the Crown, for non-appearance to meet a disreputable charge before the High Commission at Lambeth, 'two several bonds one of one hundred pounds and the other of fyfty pounds', these were bestowed upon Orlando Gibbons by the king 'for and in consideration of the good and faythfull service heretofore done unto ourselfe by Orlando Gibbons our organist and for divers

---

[1] Overseers' Books and Walcott's *Westminster*, quoted by Rimbault in *The Old Cheque Book of the Chapel Royal*, pp. 202–3; and in *Notes and Queries*, 3rd Series, vol. x, p. 182.

[2] *Domestic State Papers, James I*, vol. lxvii, No. 140.

[3] Ibid., *Sign Manuals*, vol. v, p. 38.

other good causes and consideracons us thereunto movinge. . . .'

In 1619 in succession to Walter Earle he was appointed 'one of his Maties, Musicians for the virginalles to attend in his highnes privie Chamber' at a salary of £46,[1] and he already held another post of a similar kind for which he received 'as one of his highnes musicions' a further salary of £40. In connexion with this latter appointment a signed receipt for £10 as a quarter's salary, dated the 1st February 1619, is to be seen in the British Museum;[2] the signature on this document is unquestionably the autograph of the composer. A similar receipt, dated the 23rd February 1617 with autograph partly mutilated, is in the Royal College of Music Library.[3]

An incident is recorded[4] in which Gibbons was the unfortunate victim of some rough handling. In September 1602 complaint was made against Henry Eveseed, a Yeoman of the Vestry, for drunkenness and that he 'did violently and sodenly without cause runne uppon Mr Gibbons took him up and threw him doune upon a standard . . . and withall he tare his band from his neck'.

Gibbons was an intimate friend of the younger Sir Christopher Hatton. Hatton was his patron and he seems to have spent a good deal of time at his splendid

---

[1] Audit Office Declared Accounts.   [2] B.M. Add. MS. 33965.
[3] R.C.M. MS. 2187.
[4] *The Old Cheque Book of the Chapel Royal*, ed. Rimbault, p. 101.

town house in Ely Place, Holborn. In the preface to his set of madrigals, published in 1612, Gibbons says they were mostly composed at Hatton's house. Gibbons could scarcely have been resident there, but he may have been a non-resident household musician to Hatton, having a room set apart for his use.

On the 17th May 1622 Camden founded the history lecture in the University of Oxford. He made his friend Heyther bearer of the deed of endowment. In return for this the university complimented Heyther by making him a Doctor of Music although he was no musician. Gibbons's anthem 'O clap your hands together' was used to serve as Heyther's exercise. At a later date Heyther founded a music lecture at Oxford and endowed it with the sum of £17. 6s. 8d. Orlando Gibbons was made a Doctor of Music on the same day as Heyther. A score of this anthem, formerly in the possession of the late Dr. W. H. Cummings and now in the Fitzwilliam Museum at Cambridge, is endorsed 'Mr Heather's Commencement Song'. This score belonged to William Gostling of Canterbury in the eighteenth century and was probably prepared from an earlier set of part-books, also belonging to Gostling, now at York Minster, in which the several voice-parts of this anthem are similarly endorsed. Wood referred to the incident in the following terms:[1] 'the song of 6 parts or more which was performed in the act for Will: Heather was

---

[1] *Fasti Oxonienses*, ed. Bliss, vol. i, p. 404.

composed by him (Gibbons), as one or more eminent musicians then living have several times told me. This Orlando was accounted one of the rarest musicians and organists of his time.'

It was in 1623 that Gibbons was appointed organist of Westminster Abbey in succession to John Parsons and he officiated at the funeral of James I; on that occasion he received, as senior organist of the Chapel Royal, an allowance of nine yards of 'blackes' and two yards for his servant.[1]

A glimpse of this great man at work in the abbey is afforded by John Hacket[2] in his description of the visit of the French envoys to make the preliminary arrangements for the betrothal of Charles, then Prince of Wales, to Princess Henrietta Maria of France. On entering the 'Door of the Quire', Hacket tells us, they heard the organ 'touch'd by the best Finger of the Age', that of Orlando Gibbons.

There is preserved in the Muniment Room at Westminster Abbey a bill, dated 1625, for certain repairs to the organ, endorsed in the autograph of Gibbons in the following terms: 'Mr Ierland I know this bill to be very resonable for I have alredy Cut him off ten shillings therefore I pray despathe him for he hath delt honestly wth ye Church Soe shall I rest yr Servant—Orlando Gibbons.'

---

[1] *The Old Cheque Book of the Chapel Royal*, ed. Rimbault, p. 156.
[2] *Scrinia reserata*, by John Hacket, pt. i, p. 210.

FACSIMILE OF A BILL AT WESTMINSTER ABBEY WITH AUTOGRAPH ENDORSEMENT

The circumstances in which Gibbons was summoned to Canterbury and there met with his death have been related with no little confusion and inaccuracy by almost all musical historians. It has been generally asserted that Gibbons was commissioned to write special music 'for the nuptials' of Charles I at Canterbury and summoned to attend there; and that during his stay he met with a fatal illness and died suddenly. In the first place it must be clearly stated that the marriage of Charles I and Henrietta Maria took place in Paris on the 1st May 1625,[1] and at this ceremony Charles was represented by the Duke of Buckingham as his proxy. Subsequently there was considerable delay in the queen's journey to England, and this was due in the main to the discontent of Parliament with reference to the large dowry demanded by the French king and to much consequent haggling. On the 31st May Charles set out from London to Canterbury to await the arrival of his bride at Dover. As she was expected to travel with much pomp and ceremony (her retinue actually numbered upwards of 4,000 souls when she landed), it was important that Charles should be in a position to greet her with all the available trappings of royal estate; and not the least among these was the 'Chapel Royal', a term which denoted not only the

[1] All the dates given here in this connexion are according to the 'old style'; 1st May and 5th June were Sundays. 11th May, the date sometimes given for the wedding, is according to the 'new style'.

whole personnel of the establishment but the vest-ments, ornaments, plate, books, and everything belong-ing to it. Thus every member of the chapel was summoned to Canterbury, and not Gibbons only. For example, Nathaniel Giles, then organist of St. George's Chapel, Windsor, was granted special leave of absence by the Windsor Chapter on the 20th May 1625 in the following terms: 'In isto capitulo viginti dies conce-duntur doctori Giles in quibus licet abesse a choro ultra dies in Statutis allocatas quia profecturus erat ad Cantu-ariam cum tota regia capella quando rex noster Carolus obviam ibat reginae suae ex Gallia transfretanti.'[1] The custom of taking the whole of the Chapel Royal when the sovereign travelled in state was one of old standing, and it was followed by great noblemen and bishops in medieval times. It was not for any particular ceremony that the Chapel attended the king on this occasion, but simply that the king's own choir might perform the daily choral services in such a manner as befitted his royal dignity, and the services were held in the cathedral, the cathedral choir no doubt joining forces with the singers of the Chapel Royal. There was certainly no special nuptial ceremony in the cathedral on this occa-sion. The queen arrived at Dover on Sunday the 12th June and spent the night there. The next morning the king journeyed from Canterbury to Dover to meet her.[2]

[1] Chapter Acts, St. George's Chapel.
[2] *Domestic State Papers, Charles I*, vol. iii, Nos. 69 and 73.

After a State dinner at midday Charles with his bride came back to Canterbury and a grand public banquet was given in the evening, 'their Majesties', as the Venetian ambassador reported, 'being waited on by the king's attendants only, to the disgust of the French who considered themselves excluded prematurely'.[1] The king and queen spent that night and the next at Canterbury, and on the 15th June they left for London.

There is but scanty reference to the royal visit among the records of the Dean and Chapter of Canterbury. In the Treasurer's accounts[2] for 1625 among the 'Feoda et Regarda' (fees and 'tips') is the item 'officiariis dn̄ nr̄ı Regis Caroli in adventu eius pd̄e (praedictae) ecclesiae ex mera benevolentia dc̄orū (dictorum) decani et ca˜li eisdem officiariis dat(æ) xxxli'. Again, among 'Expensae Necessariae' 'pro auratura baculorum de le canopie Regis ad duas vices xlvis . . . pro conservacione portus Australis et borealis ad diversas vices, viz. tempore praesentie Regis Caroli, tempore nundinarum, et tempore pestilentie liiis vid'. . . 'pro emendacione organorum in adventu Regis xxs'. . . 'pulsatoribus Campanarum eodem tempore xxxs'.

No doubt the king would have been present in the cathedral at the Sunday services during his stay at Canterbury, thus the Treasurer's accounts indicate that some sort of gorgeous seat with a canopy was pre-

---

[1] *Venetian State Papers*, 1625–6, 114 and 125.

[2] Communicated by Rev. Dr. A. J. Mason, Canon of Canterbury.

pared for his attendance; a special peal of bells would have certainly greeted the arrival of the royal pair from Dover.

Such then were the circumstances of the visit of Gibbons with the Chapel Royal to Canterbury. He would have arrived there, like Giles, in the last week in May, and it is not impossible that he composed special music to be used on the Sundays during the king's residence, although there is no record of his being commissioned to write anything. It is noteworthy that Ascension Day, Whit-Sunday, and Trinity Sunday fell on the 26th May, the 5th June, and the 12th June respectively, and it is quite possible that the anthem 'Grant, Holy Trinity', which is a prayer for the King, was composed for this Trinity Sunday; 'O God the King of Glory' is another anthem which may have been written for Canterbury.

On Whit-Sunday, the 5th June, Gibbons was suddenly seized with an apoplectic fit and died. He was buried on the following day in Canterbury Cathedral, as duly recorded in the burial register.

His death is recorded in the Cheque Book of the Chapel Royal as follows:[1]

'Mr. Orlando Gibbons organist, died the 5th of June being then Whitsonday at Canterbury wher the Kinge was then to receave Queene Mary who was then to com out of Fraunce and Thomas Warwick was sworne in his place organist the first daie of July following and to receave the pay of the pistoler.'

[1] *The Old Cheque Book of the Chapel Royal*, ed. Rimbault, p. 11.

Warwick also succeeded Gibbons in his other Court appointments. A warrant dormant 'under ye Signett to the Trēr of the Chamber' provides for payment 'to Thomas Warwick gent during his life two severall Annuities of 46^li and 40^li for the exercise of two severall places of his Maties, Musicions In such manner as Orlando Gibbons deceased lat^y had enjoied ye same during his life. By order of ye Lo: Chamberlaine, 25 June 1625'.[1]

Gibbons's sudden death must have caused a sensation among his fellow musicians, but it created no small alarm in Court circles, for sudden death was generally associated with the plague. John Chamberlain writes to Sir Dudley Carleton on the 12th June 1625: 'That wch makes us the more afraid is that the sickness increaseth so fast . . . Orlando Gibbon the organist of the chappell (that had the best hand in England) died the last weeke at Caunterburie not wth out suspicion of the sicknes.'[2] But the Court officials had already taken steps to ascertain the truth about this case. On the day after his death Drs. Poe and Domingo were called on by 'Mr. Secretarie Morton' to make a report 'touchinge the musitian that dyed at Canterburie and suggested to have the plague'; their report[3] was as follows:

'Wee whose names are heere underwrytten: having beene called to give o^r counsailes to Mr. Orlando Gibbons; in the tyme of his

---

[1] *State Papers, Docquets,* 1625. Calendared in Appendix, vol. i, car. i.
[2] *Domestic State Papers, Charles I,* 1625, vol. iii, No. 60.
[3] Ibid., vol. iii, No. 37.

late & suddaine sicknes, wch wee found to be in the beginning, lethargicall, or a profound sleep: out of w^{ch}, wee could never recover him, neyther by inward nor outward medicines, & then instantly he fell in most strong, & sharp convulsions: wch did wring his mouth up to his eares, & his eyes were distorted, as though they would have beene thrust out of his head & then suddenly he lost both speach, sight, & hearing, & so grew apoplecticall & lost the whole motion of every part of his body, & so died . . . we carefully viewed the bodye, wch wee found also to be very cleene wth out any show or spott of any contagious matter.'

It will be noticed that the statement that smallpox was the cause of his death is wholly devoid of foundation, but it has been repeated by several historians.

A monumental tablet was placed on the wall of the north aisle of the nave of Canterbury Cathedral, surmounted by a coat of arms and bust and bearing the following inscription:

ORLANDO GIBBONIO CAN̄TABRIGIÆ IN̄TER MVSAS ET MVSICÆ NATO
SACRÆ R CAPELLÆ ORGANISTÆ SPHÆRARVMQ HARMONIÆ
DIGITORVM PVLSV ÆMVLO
CAN̄TIONVM COMPLVRIVM QVÆQ EVM NON CANVN̄T MINVS
QVAM CANVN̄TVR CONDITORI
VIRO IN̄TEGERRIMO ET CVIVS VITA CVM ARTE SVAVISSIMIS MORIBVS
CONCORDISSIME CERTAVIT
AD NVPT C R CVM M B DOROBERN ACCITO ICTVQ HEV SANGVINIS
CRVDO ET CRVDELI FATO EXTINCTO CHOROQ COELESTI TRANSCRIPTO
DIE PEN̄TECOSTES A D N MDC XXV
ELIZABETHA CONIVX SEPTEMQ EX EO LIBERORVM PARENS
TAN̄TI VIX DOLORIS SVPERSTES MEREN̄TISS⁰ MÆREN̄TISSᴬ P
VIXIT A . . . M . . . D . . .

MONUMENT TO ORLANDO GIBBONS IN
CANTERBURY CATHEDRAL

The inscription was printed in Dart's *History of Canterbury*[1] and in part by Hawkins[2] and others, but in each case several inaccuracies have occurred. In some cases *musicam* is substituted for *musicae*, and even Ouseley followed the common error, found also in Hawkins, of printing *maerentissimo* for *merentissimo*. The final three letters stand for Annos, Menses, Dies, but unfortunately the spaces left for the figures, which should have given his exact age to a day, were never filled in. The drafting of the inscription in other ways is misleading, and shows signs of careless work. The bust of the composer is a fine one, but unfortunately it has suffered from rough usage and the nose is broken. The engraving given by Dart[3] is a miserable bit of work and in no way represents the original. This engraving was unfortunately reproduced in connexion with the Gibbons Commemoration in Westminster Abbey on the 5th June 1907, on which occasion a copy of the Canterbury bust was placed in the Abbey.

The coat of arms is or, a lion rampant sable, depressed by a bend gules, charged with three escallops argent. Dart described this correctly, but substituted crescents for escallops in his engraving of the monument.

Gibbons died intestate. Letters of administration were granted to his widow Elizabeth by the Dean and

---

[1] Dart's *History and Antiquities of Canterbury*, pp. 51–2.
[2] Hawkins, *History of Music*, vol. iv, p. 32.
[3] Dart, op. cit., p. 52.

Chapter of Westminster[1] on the 13th July 1626, more than thirteen months after his death. Legal procedure establishes the fact that the widow must have been living at that date. The statement[2] that her will was proved on the 30th July 1626 cannot well be correct; it is not accompanied by any reference, nor can its author recollect the source of his information; an exhaustive search for this will has proved abortive. Nevertheless it would seem to be true that Orlando's widow did not long survive him, and his family appear to have gathered round Edward Gibbons at Exeter. The Elizabeth Gibbons who was buried at St. Margaret's, Westminster, on the 2nd July 1626 cannot possibly have been Orlando's widow.

A portrait of Gibbons is in the Examination Schools at Oxford. It was presented to the Music School by Dr. Philip Hayes shortly before 1795. It is a copy of a contemporary portrait now lost, but belonging formerly to Mrs. Fussell, widow of Peter Fussell, organist of Winchester Cathedral, the pupil and successor of James Kent.

Orlando Gibbons had three sons and four daughters, all of whom were baptized at St. Margaret's, Westminster. James, baptized on the 2nd June 1607, died in infancy and was buried on the 4th June. Christopher was baptized on the 22nd August 1615; Orlando on the

---

[1] D. and C. of Westminster, Wills, 1626, A. III. 104 (now at Somerset House).　　　　[2] *Dict. Nat. Biog.* sub Orlando Gibbons.

29th August 1623; Alice on the 5th August 1613; Ann on the 6th October 1618; Mary on the 9th April 1621; and Elizabeth on the 16th March 1622. It is possible that Ann is to be identified with the Ann Gibbons who married William Stocke at St. Margaret's, Westminster, on the 20th December 1647. Mary married —— Soper, and Elizabeth —— Greenslade; on the 9th August 1650 these two were jointly granted letters of administration of the estate of their brother Orlando,[1] who died unmarried that year and was resident at Exeter at the time of his death. Both these sisters were married before 1650. The names of Soper and Greenslade are fairly common in the neighbourhood of Exeter and it is likely that lineal descendants of Orlando Gibbons may be traced through his daughters.

CHRISTOPHER GIBBONS

Christopher, Orlando's son, was a musician of some note. It should be mentioned that a 'Chrystopher Gybbuns' was buried at St. Margaret's, Westminster, on the 5th June 1562; beyond the coincidence of the names, which calls forth the slender suggestion that he may have been father or uncle of Orlando's father, there is no evidence to connect him with the family of musicians. Christopher, son of Orlando, was born, as already stated, in 1615; it seems likely that he was named after his uncle, Christopher Edmondes, or possibly

[1] P.C.C. Admons 1650.

after Orlando's patron, Sir Christopher Hatton. He received his early musical training as one of the children of the Chapel Royal. He was ten years old at the time of his father's death and is said to have been adopted by his uncle, Edward Gibbons, at Exeter. If it were the case, he would have had Matthew Locke as a companion of his boyhood, and it was Locke with whom in later years he collaborated in the production of a musical setting of Shirley's masque, *Cupid and Death*. In 1638 he became organist of Winchester Cathedral. On the 23rd September 1646 at St. Bartholomew-the-Less he married Mary, daughter of Dr. Robert Kercher, a prebendary of Winchester, and on the 28th February 1661 Gibbons petitioned the king 'for a letter to the Dean and Chapter of Winchester Cathedral to obtain him his tenant right in virtue of his marriage with Mary dau. of Dr. Kercher a late prebendary to a tenement in Whitchurch Manor belonging to the cathedral now held by John Campian who obtained it during the war'.[1] Mrs. Gibbons died in 1662 and was buried in the north cloister of Westminster Abbey on the 15th April of that year.[2] There seem to have been no children of this marriage. Gibbons married secondly Elizabeth, daughter of —— Ball. In a note in the Harleian Society's vol. x. 206, it is stated that her will leaves it uncertain whether Ball was her maiden name or that of a former husband;

[1] *Cal. of Domestic State Papers, Charles II*, vol. xxxi, p. 65.
[2] Harl. Soc., vol. x, p. 156.

this statement is repeated in the *Dictionary of National Biography* sub Chr. Gibbons. The will[1] shows beyond all doubt that it was her maiden name. She survived her husband six years and left three children, Elizabeth, Anne, and Mary, all living in 1678 when the will was executed. She was buried on the 27th December 1682 in the abbey cloisters near her husband in accordance with the wish expressed in her will; there can be little doubt that, as stated in Chester's Westminster Abbey Registers,[2] the entry 'Elizabeth Bull' on the 27th December 1682 refers to her.

While Gibbons was at Winchester the Civil War broke out, and in 1644 it is said that he joined the Royalist Army. At the Restoration he was rewarded for his services by the appointments of organist of the Chapel Royal, private organist to Charles II and organist of Westminster Abbey. On the 2nd July 1663 the king addressed the Vice-Chancellor of Oxford University recommending that Christopher Gibbons, organist of the Chapel Royal, who had served from his youth and was well skilled in the science of music, should be admitted to the degree of Doctor of Music on condition of his performing the usual exercises and paying his fees.[3] He died on the 20th October 1676 and was buried in the abbey cloisters. It would seem from the statements made in his widow's will that the 'merry

---

[1] P.C.C. 4 Drax.   [2] Harl. Soc., vol. x, p. 206 *note*.
[3] *Domestic State Papers, Charles II*, vol. lxxvi, p. 12 (Ent. Book 12, p. 24).

monarch' owed him 'for his services £279. 10s. 0d. or thereabouts', and this sum was still unpaid by the 'Office of his Majesty's Treasury Chamber' in 1677.[1]

Christopher left no actual will; but an 'admon. cum testō nuncupativo', or nuncupative will, dated 'on or about 17th October 1676', was proved on the 6th November following by his widow Elizabeth, who was thus authorized to dispose of his property 'for the maintenance of herself and children'.[2]

Both as a practical musician and as a composer Christopher Gibbons fell very far short of his father. Some confusion between the two has arisen in late-seventeenth-century manuscripts in the case of certain compositions; for example, the anthem 'Why seek ye the living?' is sometimes ascribed to Orlando though it is Christopher's work. It is probable also that the anthem 'Sing we merrily', the manuscript organ-score of which is at Christ Church, Oxford,[3] is by Christopher. Confusion between father and son is also to be found in their instrumental work. Christopher wrote a very large number of string fantasies of two parts; some of these are wrongly ascribed to Orlando in the catalogue of Marsh's Library, Dublin. It should be noted that in seventeenth-century manuscripts Christopher was very generally described as 'Dr Gibbons', whereas his father's name very rarely has any degree attached to it.

---

[1] Will of Elizabeth Gibbons, P.C.C. 4 Drax.
[2] P.C.C. 140 Bence.   [3] Ch. Ch. MS. 1230, f. 441.

The name of Richard Gibbons is appended to two manuscript four-part string fantasies in Marsh's Library, Dublin.[1] These same fantasies are in manuscript in the Bodleian Library,[2] but there the ascription is given in six cases as 'Mʳ R. Gibbons' and in the remaining two as 'Mʳ Gibbons'. The compiler of the Bodleian Summary Catalogue assumed that R. stood for Roland, and concluded without further evidence that this was Orlando Gibbons. The Marsh manuscript clearly shows that R stands for Richard, but it is possible that in both cases Gibbons may be an error for Gibbs, for Richard Gibbs was organist of Norwich Cathedral *circa* 1622–30. The two manuscripts may quite likely have a common origin. If, however, Richard Gibbons is the correct name of the composer of these two fantasies, nothing whatever is known of his personal history, and he does not seem to belong to the same family as Orlando.

[1] Z. 3. Tab. 4. 1–6.   [2] MS. Mus. Sch. C. 64–9.

CHAPTER III

Church Music

THE name of Orlando Gibbons has always been, and will continue to be, associated primarily with his Church music. It is remarkable that, as far as is known, he wrote nothing for the Latin rites of the Church, neither masses nor motets. A suggestion was at one time put forward that all the English anthems of this period were in the first instance set to Latin words, and that they first appeared in English in translations furnished by Barnard in 1641 in his book of *Selected Church Musick*. The originator of this suggestion has long ago acknowledged his error with great frankness, yet, as it was given very wide circulation, there are still many who cling to the belief that Gibbons's 'Hosanna' was originally composed for Latin words and that 'Barnard adapted them to a poor translation'. It must be said quite plainly that there is plenty of early text of this anthem and that the English version is found in every instance; the words are a conflate of Matt. xxi. 9 and Luke xix. 38 in the version of the Genevan Bible of 1557 which was still in common use in Gibbons's day, but the phrase 'blessed

be the *Kingdom* that cometh' is introduced from Mark
xi. 10. It should be observed also that although the
opening passages of the music fit the Latin version, the
difficulty of fitting the Latin text to some of the later
phrases is almost insuperable. Some Latin motets by
Tallis, Tye, Byrd, and others, were certainly adapted
to English words, but this was done in most instances
long before the days of Barnard, very generally in the
lifetime of the composers, presumably with their sanc-
tion if not actually by their own hands. In this connexion the important Edwardine manuscript in the Bodleian Library[1] may be cited for examples of original
English compositions existing even at that early date,
as well as the English adaptations of two of the Taverner
Masses, possibly, as recent research seems to show, in
Taverner's own hand.

Gibbons was scarcely forty-two years old at the
time of his death, but his musical output was not a very
large one as compared with that of Byrd: his English
Church music that is known to survive today consists
of two sets of preces and psalms, two services, some
forty anthems, and seventeen hymn-tunes. The anthems may be considered first. As an anthem-writer
Gibbons stands at the cross-ways. When writing in the
polyphonic style he was looking back to the splendid
traditions which had been built up during the sixteenth
century, to reach their full measure of development and

[1] Bodl. MSS. Mus. Sch. E. 420-2.

perfection at the close of Elizabeth's reign. In the work of Byrd not only all that was best in the conventional musical forms of the old Latin services was summed up, but a new model had also been designed and perfected for dealing with the newly established English services as contained in the Book of Common Prayer. Further development was not possible in the polyphonic style, either with Latin or English subjects. Gibbons could follow this style, and did so with splendid success; and indeed his purely polyphonic work, as exhibited in 'Hosanna', 'O clap your hands', 'Lift up your heads', and 'Lord in thy wrath', places him without question in the highest rank of the English polyphonic composers. But the great artist is he who can quickly perceive that a traditional form is worked out, and can, with the knowledge that all true art is based upon progress, look forward as well as back, and so break new ground. In doing so he may succeed in bringing to perfection something that is new in character; he may, however, either fail completely, or do no more than prepare a new way in which full success will be achieved, not by himself but by those who come after him. In this latter instance the high merit of his endeavours must not be overlooked, for without his pioneer work later successes might never have been won. If Gibbons looked back, he also looked forward, and his efforts in exploring the possibilities of the verse anthem and in preparing the way for Blow, Pelham Humphrey, and

Purcell should earn for him the highest commendation, even though few of his verse anthems can be regarded as first-rate works of art.

Not counting the three psalms which were especially attached to his settings of the preces, there are forty anthems of Gibbons known today. Of ten of these only incomplete parts have hitherto been found, and the complete score of these cannot satisfactorily be reconstructed. No more than fifteen out of the forty are written in the polyphonic style; the rest are 'verse' anthems, namely, compositions in which there are passages for solo voices with independent accompaniment either for organ or strings. This apparent preference on the part of Gibbons for the new style of composition comes as something of a surprise to those whose knowledge of his works has usually been limited to some half a dozen of them, and have supposed him to be exclusively a polyphonic composer.

The fifteen polyphonic anthems, as already stated, show Gibbons to be in the very first rank of the great school of English composers of whom he was the youngest and, with the exception of Tomkins, practically the last. Until recently only those anthems have been generally known in cathedral circles which were selected by Boyce for inclusion in his *Cathedral Music* in the eighteenth century; and of these 'O clap your hands' and 'Lift up your heads' were seldom sung even in the cathedrals. Familiarity with his anthems was thus for long reduced to two: namely, 'Almighty and everlasting God' and 'Hosanna'. These two works, representing two sharply contrasted styles, are, as it happens, in Gibbons's very best manner; and for this reason they alone have served successfully in keeping his great name alive and in sustaining his reputation at a high level through the long period of more than two centuries during which Tudor music suffered wholesale neglect.

'Almighty and everlasting God' is an ideal setting of a collect, but it is not easy to sing well, for the contrapuntal character of the writing gives great independence to the individual outline of the several parts and calls for very careful interpretation; at no point throughout the anthem do all the four parts come together with the same word until the final cadence. This characteristic is a marked feature of almost all Gibbons's polyphonic work, secular and sacred alike, and he introduces far fewer homophonic sections than perhaps any other of the Tudor composers. Charles Burney mentions this characteristic of Gibbons's work and says[1] that the 'purists' of his day 'on account of the confusion arising from all parts singing different words at the same time, pronounce the style, in which his full anthems are composed, to be vicious'. Burney himself disagreed with this criticism, and added in reference to the anthems that 'the lovers of fugue, ingenious contri-

[1] Burney's *General History of Music*, vol. iii, p. 330.

vance, and rich, simple, and pleasing harmony, must regard them as admirable productions'. The secret of singing music of this complex character with proper effect is to be found in giving special care to the selection of the syllables in each phrase that call for accentuation, and, conversely, those that should be lightened; it will be found that the latter class largely preponderates, and consequently the syllables and notes that should be stressed with varying degrees of intensity will stand out, now in this part and now in that, above the musical texture as a whole, and clarity will then take the place of confusion.

'Hosanna' is too well known to call for much comment, but attention should be drawn to the form on which it is constructed and especially to the recapitulation of the opening subject. In all the early texts the opening phrase in the lowest part is assigned to a second tenor; this evidently represents the composer's intention, and the same point is repeated in the recapitulation of this passage near the end of the anthem. It was Boyce who first assigned this entry to the bass voices. Some early texts also give the opening passage and some subsequent sections to 'verse', or solo voices; the contrast thus obtained adds much to the effect of the anthem. These indications are incorporated in the Carnegie 8vo edition of this anthem.[1] The free triple

---

[1] *Hosanna to the Son of David*, Gibbons, ed. by E. H. Fellowes. Oxford University Press.

rhythm with which this anthem opens must not be hampered in performance by the presence of the bar-lines; these must inevitably sever the phrase here and there in one voice or another because of the contra-puntal character of the writing. The anthem has frequently been spoilt by failure to observe the true rhythmic outline of the phrases.

Other unaccompanied anthems designed on a big scale are 'Lift up your heads' which is rather similar to 'Hosanna', especially in the opening phrase, and 'O clap your hands' with its second part 'God is gone up'. This was the anthem which Heather was allowed to use for his degree at Oxford in 1622. Except for a single tenor-part the Gostling books at York provide the earliest known text of this anthem. It was not printed by Barnard in 1641, but Boyce included it in his *Cathedral Music*. In the opening of the *Gloria Patri*, with which it ends, there are some perplexing puzzles connected with the rules of *musica ficta*; if the F on the word *be* is sharpened in every case, some curious clashes will occur at certain points. Boyce has copied one obvious small error in the York text; at the first entry of the words 'God sitteth upon his holy seat' in the second tenor part the word 'holy' should be set to F G, not G G.

'O Lord in thy wrath' is a beautiful anthem, and, being penitential in character, is in sharp contrast with the vigorous exuberance of the three anthems just mentioned. Another penitential anthem is 'O Lord in thee is all my trust'; this five-part anthem is in many respects characteristic of Gibbons; but it is a little drawn out in length and it loses something owing to the inferiority of the words which are in the form of a metrical hymn described in the manuscript[1] as 'A Lamentation'. It is unfortunate that no more than a single bass part and a sketchy organ-score have been found of 'Out of the deep'; this has all the appearance of being a very fine work.

'O Lord, increase my faith' is a little gem written for four voices, and there are three or four more written on a similar scale; among these are 'O Lord, how do my woes' and 'O Lord, I lift my heart to thee'; these two were alone of all Gibbons's anthems printed in his lifetime; they were included by Leighton in his *Teares or Lamentacions of a Sorrowfull Soule*, published in 1614.

Passing to the verse anthems it must be frankly admitted we find ourselves on a decidedly lower level. Gibbons was, of course, not the originator of the verse anthem; several examples of this kind of composition are to be found in Byrd's work, and some at least of these must have been written long before Gibbons grew to manhood; but he is perhaps to be regarded as the most important pioneer of this form of anthem, and all praise is due to him for his enterprise in exploring new fields when he could have remained in the tried regions of polyphonic music in which he scored such

[1] Ch. Ch., Oxford, MS. 21.

splendid successes. Gibbons was in this sense a true member of the Elizabethan School, for he proved that the spirit of enterprise, so vital in that school, was by no means wholly spent even in the less inspiring atmosphere of King James's reign. But the music of these anthems has to be judged in a detached manner apart from any considerations of this kind, and a very large portion of it must thus inevitably be placed no higher than the second class. Three or four of these anthems, however, stand out conspicuously above the rest of this list. For example, 'This is the record of John' is a very remarkable piece of work; it takes the form of a narrative given to a solo voice; the narrative is divided into three sections, at the close of each of which the chorus repeats some of the words already declaimed by the soloist. The chorus at its first entry takes up the concluding phrase of the solo, but varies the melodic material in an ingenious manner; the curious and characteristic *roulade* of the solo is reflected in a highly artistic manner at the cadence in the first alto part. The second choral section repeats the whole of the words just declaimed by the soloist, but in the final section the concluding words only are repeated. Considered both from a melodic and a declamatory point of view, the solo part is a masterly bit of work and far ahead of anything that had been written before that date. The accompaniment is also of much interest, and was written originally for strings. 'This Anthem', as stated in the Christ Church MS., 'was made for Dr Laud president of Saint John's College.' The word *Oxford* is added in a later hand.

In the same manuscript[1] are ten more verse anthems, all of which have an accompaniment for viols. This manuscript was for many years believed to be in Gibbons's autograph; the belief was founded on a statement in Benjamin Rogers's hand pasted in on a slip at the beginning of the volume and worded thus: 'Ben Rogers his booke Aug: 18. 1673 and p̄sented me by Mr John Playford stationer in the Temple London. This Score booke was done formerly by that rare Musition, Mr Orlando Gibbons and this book is of great value to a Composer.' The exact meaning of this inscription is in itself a little obscure, but on internal evidence there seems little likelihood that the manuscript was written by Gibbons. All the headings are admittedly in another hand, that of Rogers. The volume contains: (1) the nine three-part fantasies of Gibbons and on fo. 17 is written 'The end of Mr Gibbons 3 parts for ye viols'; (2) three six-part fantasies by Orlando Gibbons; (3) three three-part fantasies by Christopher Gibbons in a later hand; (4) 'Mr Orlando Gibons his songes of 5 Partes' (this is the madrigal set, complete without any words); (5) 'Awake my soul', no composer named; (6) Fantasies by Coperario; (7) two anthems in Rogers's autograph; (8) eleven verse anthems by Orlando

[1] Ch. Ch., Oxford, MS. 21.

Gibbons; (9) madrigals by Nenna, &c., in a later hand. Sections 1, 2, 4, 5, 6, and 8 of the volume are in the same hand, and this fact in itself seems against the theory that it is Gibbons's; the hand is more characteristic of a musical scribe than of a composer; the errors in No. 9 are so many and of such a character that it is almost inconceivable they were written by the composer. Finally a comparison with the undoubted signatures of Gibbons on receipts for his salary,[1] as well as the autograph endorsement on the bill preserved at Westminster Abbey, seems conclusive in proving that MS. 21 is not in the hand of Orlando Gibbons, although it has great value as text.

Among the Gibbons anthems in this Christ Church MS. are 'Behold thou hast made', which was written for the funeral of Anthony Maxey, Dean of Windsor, in 1618; 'This Anthem was made at the entretie of Doctor Maxcie Deane of Windsor the same day sennight before his death.'[2] 'Great King of Gods', 'made for the King's being in Scotland'[2] in 1617; 'Blessed are all they', written for the wedding of Lord Somerset and the notorious Lady Essex in 1613; and 'O all true faithful hearts', written for a thanksgiving service held at Paul's Cross on the 1st June 1619 for the king's recovery from sickness. This last anthem was adapted by Ouseley to words specially written for him by Rev. H. R. Bramley,

[1] B.M. Add. MS. 33965. R.C.M., MS. 2187.
[2] Ch. Ch. MS. 21.

beginning 'O thou the central orb', and it is now very generally sung to these words.

Among the more effective verse anthems of Gibbons besides 'This is the record' are 'Almighty God who by thy Son' (the St. Peter's Day Collect), and 'O God the King of Glory'.

Only two services of Orlando Gibbons exist today and there is no indication of his having written others. Curiously enough, they represent his two styles of Church music; the well-known F service is purely polyphonic and the D minor is a 'Verse' service with an independent organ accompaniment. And just as the two classes of anthems represent two standards of artistic attainment, so it is with the services. The shorter polyphonic service is in the first class, but the verse service, though it contains some fine passages, is no more than a splendid experiment. In design the F service follows the usual convention at that date; like the Byrd services, it begins with *Venite*, although the settings of that canticle must very shortly afterwards have given place to a chant in daily cathedral usage; and this is followed by *Te Deum, Benedictus, Kyrie,* Creed, *Magnificat,* and *Nunc Dimittis.* It is written on the lines of the 'short' services of the Elizabethans, but in comparison with the 'short service' of Byrd, which is very largely homophonic, Gibbons's work is far more complex; it is full of imitative treatment and the voices rarely come together at the same word; yet the words run on with little repetition. Good results of Gibbons's ingenuity in dealing with complex imitative are figures provided at the words 'We therefore pray thee help thy servants' in the *Te Deum*; 'And thou, child' in the *Benedictus* and 'Abraham and his seed' in the *Magnificat*. Of the canon in the *Gloria* to the *Nunc Dimittis* Burney[1] said he could discover in it 'no restraint or stiffness in the melody, which continues to move with the same freedom, as if no *canon* had existence'. Of the many beautiful features of this service perhaps none surpass the final passage of this *Gloria*. One peculiar phrase in the *Magnificat* calls for mention: a scale of quavers is written for the second syllable of the word 'servant' in the treble part; the whole passage in this voice part, beginning with the words 'He rememb'ring', is in triple rhythm, but the words have been wrongly underlaid by Boyce and those editors who followed his text; consequently the flow of the rhythm was wrongly disturbed where the scale comes. With reference to this passage it is necessary to make a slight digression, for this scale of quavers is not the only example of its kind in Gibbons's Church music; yet nothing similar is found, as far as is known to the present writer, in the work of any other English composer quite so early as this. These phrases really correspond to the grace notes and *cadenzas* which are familiar in music of a later date. Gibbons wrote a very similar rapid scale passage for the solo voice in

[1] *A General History of Music*, vol. iii, p. 329.

'See, see, the Word is incarnate' at the words 'When now he sits on God's right hand'; here the scale consists of one note less than the octave, and it runs a minor third beyond the note to which it falls on the strong rhythmic point. The scale in these two places may possibly be intended to represent a kind of *portamento*. Two bars later, at the final cadence of the solo passage, precisely the same phrase of quavers is used as at the end of the first solo in 'This is the record of John'. Another example of this kind is to be found in the bass solo at the opening of 'Glorious and powerful God'; in both these latter instances the quick notes foreshadow the more modern *cadenza*, and they should be treated accordingly in performance. A characteristic and interesting group of four quick quavers occurs in a phrase several times repeated in 'Blessed is he that feareth the Lord'. This peculiar feature of Gibbons's writing may be compared with the *tremolo* written out in reiterated notes in some of Walter Porter's compositions; Porter's work was several years later than that of Gibbons, but he is said to have taken the idea from Monteverde.

Returning to Gibbons's service, the *Sanctus* in F, which Boyce printed as by Gibbons in his *Cathedral Music*, is spurious. It finds no place in any text of the service earlier than Boyce except in a manuscript in Child's hand at St. George's Chapel, Windsor, and to that manuscript it is a subsequent addition. After the Restoration it had become customary to sing the

Sanctus at the morning service on Sundays, and it would seem that Child had the idea to design something to go with the *Kyrie* and Creed of Gibbons's F service. A very little examination of this *Sanctus* shows that the first section is adapted from 'Holy, holy, holy' of the *Te Deum* in F, and that the second section is an adaptation of the opening passage of that *Te Deum*.

The second service, as well as that in F, was printed in Barnard's *Selected Cathedral Music*. It consists only of *Te Deum*, *Jubilate*, *Magnificat*, and *Nunc Dimittis*. Of the evening canticles there is manuscript text at Durham and Peterhouse, an organ part at Christ Church, and a few scraps elsewhere; of the morning service Barnard's is the only text, but there is an organ score of the whole work in Batten's organ book.[1] The Batten text does not altogether correspond with that of Barnard; some of the passages that are developed at great length in the vocal text are found in shortened form in the organ score; there is no means of knowing whether this shortening was the work of the composer; Batten's manuscript and Barnard's printed books were both produced within a very few years after Gibbons's death. The *Te Deum* is of considerable length. It opens, as Byrd's second evening service does, with a short passage for solo voice with organ accompaniment, followed by a trio, the full chorus entering first at the words 'To thee all Angels cry

[1] Tenbury MS. 791.

68

aloud'. There are several 'verse' passages, but in some of these it is impossible not to feel that the effects are thin, and in such a passage as 'in the Glory of the Father' it might have been supposed that at least one voice-part was missing, if it were not for the fact that the ten part-books of Barnard represent the complete text. Even in the polyphonic sections much of the writing seems unworthy of this great genius; it is difficult to explain, for example, how the bass phrase 'The holy church throughout' should have been cut off incomplete and left, as it were, hanging in the air; the protracted section at the words 'Thine honourable true and only Son' is treated in a perfunctory and conventional fashion which makes the repetitions wearisome. Yet it must be remembered that if we feel this service to be something of a failure, the composer was exploring new and uncharted seas with daring and most praiseworthy enterprise.

The *Jubilate* is one of the few examples of the musical settings of the alternative to the *Benedictus* at this date. Like the *Te Deum* it also opens with a solo voice, and it is treated in alternate sections throughout; the whole of the text is given out in the first instance by the solo voice or verse, the concluding phrases being taken up by the chorus. This represents an entirely novel method of treating the canticles at this period.

The verses of the *Magnificat* are alternately set for verse and chorus. The canticle opens with several bars for organ alone and the first verse is for two treble voices. The first and last verses of the *Nunc Dimittis* are for treble duet. The same elaborated *Amen* at the close of the *Gloria Patri* appears in both these canticles, another unusual feature at this period.

The preces and psalms call for little comment; the two sets of preces are practically identical. The text of 'Awake up my glory' is unfortunately not complete. Like Byrd's 'Lift up your heads' it is designed on the lines of an anthem. Of the other two psalms 'The eyes of all wait' is rather the more elaborate; the small opening phrase for the organ alone is worth noticing. 'I will magnify thee' follows the somewhat free chant-form used by both Tallis and Byrd, among others, which foreshadows the so-called double Anglican chant.

Gibbons made an important contribution to English Church music by writing sixteen tunes for Withers's *Hymnes and Songs of the Church*; and an extra tune is added in a manuscript at Christ Church, Oxford.[1] Many of these have been adapted for use as hymn-tunes, but the characteristic rhythms have suffered in many cases from bad editing. In their original form the treble and bass alone were given.

[1] Ch. Ch. MS. 365, f. 38.

List of Church *Music* by Orlando Gibbons

First Preces and Psalms (for Whit-Sunday at Evensong). Barnard. Durham E. 4–11, C. 1, 12, 13, 18, A. 2. Peterhouse 34, 35, 36, 37, 39, 42, 43, 44, 45.
> The eyes of all wait.
> Awake up my glory.

Second Preces and Psalm (for Easter Day at Evensong). Peterhouse 33, 34, 38, 39. Ch. Ch. 1220–4.
> I will magnify thee.

First Service in F. Barnard. B.M. Add. 17784. Durham C. 8, A. 1. Peterhouse 33, 34, 35, 36, 37, 38, 39, 42, 43, 44, 45 and Blackletter Prayer-book. R.C.M. 1045–51. Ch. Ch. 1001. Ely 4, 28. York, Windsor, Wimborne.
Venite, Te Deum, Benedictus, Kyrie, Creed, *Magnificat, Nunc Dimittis.*

Second Service in D minor with verses to the organs. Barnard. B.M. Add. 17784, 31443. Durham C. 1, 12, 13, 18, A. 2. Peterhouse 33, 34, 38, 39. Ch. Ch. 1001. Tenbury 791.
Te Deum, Jubilate, Magnificat, Nunc Dimittis.

Full Anthems.
> Almighty and everlasting God, a 4. Barnard. B.M. Add. 29289, 30478–9. Durham C. 4, 6, 9, 10, 11, 15, 16, A. 1. York, Windsor. R.C.M. 1045–7.
> { Deliver us O Lord our God, *1st part*, a 4. }
> { Blessed be the Lord God of Israel, *2nd part*, a 4. }
>> Barnard. R.C.M. 1045–51. Windsor, York.
> Hosanna to the Son of David, a 6. Barnard. B.M. Add. 17784, 30478–9. Durham C. 4, 5, 16, A. 1. York. Ch. Ch. 1001.
> *I am the Resurrection, a 5. B.M. Add. 29366–8.
> Lift up your heads, a 6. Barnard. B.M. Add. 30478–9. Durham C. 1, 2, 3, 11, 14, 16, A. 1. Peterhouse 33, 34, 38, 39. Ch. Ch. 1001. York.

* Of these the text is incomplete.

⎧O clap your hands together, 1*st part*, a 8. ⎫
⎩God is gone up with a merry noise, 2*nd part*, a 8.⎭
    B.M. Add. 29289. York.

O Lord, how do my woes, a 4. Leighton's *Teares*, &c. B.M.
    Roy. App. 63.

O Lord, I lift my heart to thee, a 5. Leighton's *Teares*, &c.
    B.M. Roy. App. 63.

O Lord, in thee is all my trust, a 5. Ch. Ch. 21.

O Lord, in thy wrath rebuke me not, a 6. R.C.M. 1045–51.

O Lord, increase my faith, a 4. B.M. Harl. 7337.

*Out of the deep, ?a 5. Ch. Ch. 1001. St. John's Coll., Oxf., 181.

Why art thou so heavy? a 4. B.M. Harl. 7337.

Verse Anthems.

*Almighty God, which hast given (Christmas Day). Ch. Ch.
    1001. Tenbury 791. St. John's Coll., Oxf., 180.

Almighty God, who by thy Son (St. Peter's Day). B.M. Add.
    30478. Durham C. 1, 2, 3, 7, 11, 16, A. 4. Lambeth 764.
    Tenbury 791. St. John's Coll., Oxf., 181.

*Arise, O Lord God. B.M. Add. 30479.

Behold, I bring you glad tidings (Christmas Day). B.M. Add.
    17784, 30478–9, 31443. Durham C. 1, 2, 3, 7, 11, 16,
    A. 2. Peterhouse 33, 34, 38, 39. R.C.M. 1045–51. Tenbury
    791. York, Windsor, Ely 1.

Behold thou hast made my days (Funeral of Dean Maxey)
    (string accpt.). Barnard. B.M. Add. 17784, 30479. Ch. Ch.
    21, 1001. Durham C. 1, 4, 6, 9, 10, 11, 16. Peterhouse 33,
    34, 38, 39. R.C.M. 1045–51. York. Tenbury 791.

Blessed are all they (for Lord Somerset's wedding) (string
    accpt.). B.M. Add. 30478. Ch. Ch. 21, 1001. Durham C.
    1, 4, 5, 6, 9, 10, 11, 16, A. 4. R.C.M. 1045–51. York.

Glorious and powerful God (string accpt.). B.M. Add. 17784,
    30478. Durham C. 1, 2, 3, 4, 5, 6, 10, 11, 14, 15, A. 2. Ch.
    Ch. 21. Peterhouse 37, 38, 43, 44, 45, 51. R.C.M. 1045–51.
    Ely 1. Tenbury 791. York, Wimborne.

Grant, Holy Trinity ('for the King's Day'). B.M. Add. 30478–9.
    Durham C. 1, 2, 3, 4, 5, 6, 7, 9, 10, 11, 14, 16, 19, A. 4. St. John's
    Coll., Oxf., 181. Tenbury 791. Ch. Ch. 1001. Lambeth 764.

Great King of Gods (for the King James be ing in Scotland (string accpt.). Ch. Ch. 21.

*Have pity upon me. B.M. Add. 30478. Durham C. 2, 3, 14.

If ye be risen again with Christ (Easter Day). B.M. Add. 30478-9. Durham C. 1, 2, 3, 11, 14, 16, A. 1. Peterhouse 33, 34, 38, 39. Ch. Ch. 1001. Tenbury 791. R.C.M. 1045-51. York.

Lord, grant grace (All Saints' Day) (string accpt.). Ch. Ch. 21.

*Lord, we beseech thee (for the Annunciation). Ch. Ch. 1001.

O all true faithful hearts (Thanksgiving for the King's recovery) (string accpt.) [adapted by Ouseley as 'O thou the central orb']. Ch. Ch. 21.

O God the King of Glory (Ascension Day). B.M. Add. 30478-9. Durham C. 1, 2, 3, 7, 11, 14, 16. Ch. Ch. 1001. St. John's Coll., Oxf., 181. Tenbury 791.

*Praise the Lord. Tenbury 791.

See, see the Word is incarnate (string accpt.). B.M. Add. 29372-6. Ch. Ch. 21, 56-60.

Sing unto the Lord (string accpt.). B.M. Add. 30478-9. Ch. Ch. 21. Durham C. 1, 4, 5, 6, 9, 10, 11, 16, 17, 19, A. 2, 5. Tenbury 791. Wimborne.

*So God loved the world (for Whit-Sunday). Tenbury 791.

The secret sins. B.M. Add. 30479. Durham C. 1, 4, 5, 6, 9, 10, 19. Tenbury 791. St. John's Coll., Oxf., 180.

This is the record of John (St. John Baptist's Day) (string accpt.). B.M. Add. 30478-9. Ch. Ch. 21. Durham C. 1, 2, 3, 4, 5, 6, 7, 9, 10, 11, 14, 16, A. 5. Peterhouse 34, 35, 37, 42, 43, 44, 46. Tenbury 791.

*Thou God of wisdom. Tenbury 791.

*Unto thee, O Lord. Tenbury 791.

We praise thee O Father (for Easter Day) (string accpt.). B.M. Add. 30478-9. Ch. Ch. 21. Durham C. 1, 2, 3, 4, 5, 6, 7, 9, 10, 11, 14, 16, A. 2. Peterhouse, 33, 34, 38, 39, 46. Tenbury 791.

Hymn tunes.

17 tunes written for Withers's *Hymnes and Songs of the Church* (1623). Ch. Ch. 365.

CHAPTER IV

Secular Vocal Music

NOTHING is more astonishing in the whole history of music than the story of the English school of madrigal composers. The long delay of its appearance, lagging behind the Italian school by no less than half a century: the suddenness of its development: the extent of the output: the variety and originality as well as the fine quality of the work: the brevity of its endurance, and the completeness with which it finally collapsed: all these features combine to distinguish the madrigal school as the strangest phenomenon in the history of English music.

It has to be remembered that music, as we commonly use the term to-day, was still in its childhood at the close of Elizabeth's reign. The seventeenth century was destined in its earliest years to see the first stages of operatic development; and when it closed Lully, Purcell, and others had brought opera to a point of healthy adolescence, but no further; and considerably more than a century was to elapse after the death of Elizabeth before the great instrumental forms, as exploited in the symphony and the string quartet, came to the birth. When Orlando Gibbons was a child opera, oratorio, symphony, and sonata were forms undreamed of; and yet one particular branch of music, that for voices singing in combination without instrumental accompaniment, had already been brought to a degree of perfection that has never since been surpassed.

During the sixteenth century there was, practically speaking, only one medium in which a composer could express his most serious thoughts, namely unaccompanied vocal music. And inasmuch as all the musical skill of Europe was concentrated upon this limited field, it followed of necessity that all the possibilities of development that could be explored under the influence of high qualities of imagination, ingenuity, and invention were rapidly worked out. It is not to be wondered at that men of towering genius such as Palestrina, Orlando di Lasso, Marenzio, and Byrd, between them, said the last word that could be said in polyphonic music in relation to the mass, the motet, the English 'service', the anthem, and the madrigal. The mine was exhausted, and as a result it may certainly be averred that even if the Civil War and the wanton acts of destruction of the mid-seventeenth century had never taken place, the period that followed the death of Orlando Gibbons and lasted until the rise of Henry Purcell would none the less have been as sterile in England as in fact it was. But the seventeenth century had run but a short way on its course before the English composers perceived clearly that they must set themselves to explore fresh paths and to discover new methods of self-expression. Some of them, like Gibbons, turned to experiment with the verse anthem, and the independent accompaniments which are a feature of it; and thus they sowed the seeds of a new kind of crop to be harvested after the Restoration. But in some notable instances the fount of composition was entirely dried up; and this was especially true of the madrigal. For example, Wilbye produced his second set of madrigals in 1609, and although he lived for nearly thirty years after that date he seems to have written nothing further except two short 'hymns' or anthems for Leighton's collection in 1614. Weelkes, as far as is known, wrote but one madrigal of first-rate importance in the last twenty-three years of his comparatively short life. Tomkins lived for thirty-four years after his book of *Songs* or madrigals was published in 1622, and wrote no more of this class of work.[1] It is remarkable, too, that Orlando Gibbons's set of madrigals was issued before he was thirty years old, and that he never wrote any others, as far as is known. The madrigal was virtually dead by 1630. After that date Martin Peerson, Walter Porter, Henry and William Lawes, among others, wrote a fair number of secular pieces for combined voices, but

---

[1] Although Tomkins survived Gibbons by thirty-one years, he was his senior in age and most of his best Church music was without doubt written before Gibbons died.

in most instances they also were breaking new ground by introducing independent instrumental accompaniment, and they seldom followed the conventional traditions of the polyphonic composers.

And following the demise of secular polyphonic song there came an incredibly long period in which English composers wrote little or nothing in this department. Blow and Purcell and the other Restoration musicians wrote a few anthems, but scarcely anything secular, on these lines; nor at a later period did Boyce. It was left to the glee-writers at the end of the eighteenth century to revive, albeit in a very inferior manner, the idea of unaccompanied secular song for combined voices; and the homophonic part-song was a product of the nineteenth century.

It was in 1612, thirteen years before his death, that Gibbons published his only set of madrigals. On the title-page he described it as his 'First Set'; but that was a convention, and several of the other madrigalists used this formula although they produced no second set. The description 'Madrigals and Mottets' on the title-page calls for some explanation; the term 'Motet' was not at that time confined, as it was later, to a sacred work with Latin words; Gibbons seems to have used it here to denote a madrigal of a serious nature in contrast to the more conventional light Elizabethan conceit. Thus he no doubt had in his mind 'What is our life?' or 'Nay let me weep' when he employed the term 'Motet', while 'Dainty fine bird' represents the madrigal. The volume was dedicated to the younger Sir Christopher Hatton.

The terms of the dedication are as follows:

SYR,

It is proportion that beautifies every thing, this whole Universe consists of it, and Musicke is measured by it, which I have endeavoured to observe in the composition of these few Ayres but cannot in their Dedication: for when I compare your many favours with my demerits, your curious Eare with these harsh Notes, there appears so plaine a disproportion betweene them, that I am afraid, least in offring to your Patronage Songs in some tune, my action herein should be out of all tune: yet I have made bould to honour them with your Name, that the world may take notice, rather of my want of abilitie, then good-will to be gratefull. By which little outward demonstration, you may easily guesse at the greatnesse of my inward affection, as skilfull Geometricians doe observe the true stature of the whole body by sight of the foote onely. Experience tels us that Songs of this Nature are usually esteemed as they are well or ill performed, which excellent grace I am sure your unequalled love unto Musicke will not suffer them to want, that the Author (whom you no lesse love) may be free from disgrace. They were most of them composed in your owne house, and doe therefore properly belong unto you, as Lord of the Soile; the language they speake you provided them, I onely furnished them with Tongues to utter the same: they are like young Schollers newly entred, that at first sing very fearefully, it requires your Patience therefore to beare with their imperfections: they were taught to sing onely to delight you, and if you shall take any pleasure in them, they have their end, and I my wish, a full recompence for my passed labours, and a greater encouragement to present you with some

future things more worthy your Patronage: till which oppor-
tunity I rest   Yours ever to command
          ORLANDO GIBBONS

The somewhat fulsome style of flattery and self-
depreciation was common to all such addresses to
patrons at this period and not confined to those of
musicians. Gibbons could no more easily abandon it
than Byrd. But the opening sentence, 'It is proportion
that beautifies everything, this whole Universe consists of it,' is a great saying; it is an axiom the truth of
which is just as unassailable today as when Gibbons
first uttered it, and it embodies a principle which should
be grasped by students in every branch of Art and
Literature. The personal references to Sir Christopher
Hatton have been variously interpreted. It must be
remembered that Gibbons's patron was not the famous
Sir Christopher Hatton who was a favourite of Queen
Elizabeth, Lord Chancellor, and a Knight of the Garter;
he, too, was a patron of Literature and Art, and Edmund
Spenser was among his protégés. It was the Lord Chancellor Hatton to whom the Bishop of Ely alienated his
splendid house, Ely Place in Holborn, under Royal
pressure, having in the first place granted him a lease of
it for twenty-one years. He died unmarried in 1591,
when the property passed first to his nephew, Sir William Newport, and later to his cousin, Sir Christopher
Hatton, who was Gibbons's friend. The younger
Hatton died in 1619.

Gibbons when he published his madrigals in 1612 was organist of the Chapel Royal, but not yet of Westminster Abbey. He was living with his wife and children in the parish of St. Margaret's, and it is not unlikely that, as already suggested, he acted as household musician to Hatton whose house was a little more than a mile distant. There can be no doubt that Gibbons consulted Hatton about the choice of the words for his madrigals, but the theory that Hatton was the author of the words was evolved from Gibbons's dedication by writers who had made no research among the works of the poets of Gibbons's day; moreover, the younger Hatton is not known to have possessed special literary gifts like his cousin and namesake. Sylvester, Spenser, Donne, and Raleigh between them account for eight out of the twenty numbers in this set, a large proportion of identifications in comparison with those in other madrigal sets. It may be inferred that Hatton selected the words for Gibbons; and that most of the music was written in Hatton's house is plainly stated in the address.

The set opens with 'The silver swan', which is possibly the best known of all English madrigals. In design this composition precisely follows the Ayre of the lutenists in its more conventional form. The cantus part is frankly melodic, and the repetition of the second limb to a further couplet of words is characteristic of the Ayres of Dowland and Campian. This lovely little piece of music will continue to rank as a first favourite for all time. The contrapuntal writing is typical of Gibbons's work and may be compared with that of the Service in F in reference to the criticism of Burney's contemporaries quoted in a former chapter;[1] thus it will be noticed that after the first four notes all the parts are singing different words except at the full close in F at the end of each of the three main sections. The chord of the augmented fifth which Gibbons used here with special effect at the word 'death' and in several of his madrigals is not found in his Church music, and for many years editors eliminated it from 'The silver swan'.

Nos. 3 to 6 together form a single composition. The words are by Joshua Sylvester and are ethical in character. This is one of the compositions which no doubt came under the heading of 'Motets' in Gibbons's mind. There is no thematic or other connexion between the four several sections of the Sylvester madrigal. Another piece of considerable length is the elegy 'Nay let me weep', which occupies three numbers in the set (17 to 19). The author of the words is not known, but they are of much beauty and may be quoted here in full:

> Nay let me weep, though others' tears be spent;
>   Though all eyes dried be, let mine be wet.
> Unto thy grave I'll pay this yearly rent,
>   Thy lifeless corse demands of me this debt.
> I owe more tears than ever corse did crave;
>   I'll pay more tears than e'er was paid to grave.

[1] p. 67.

Ne'er let the sun with his deceiving light
  Seek to make glad these watery eyes of mine.
My sorrow suits with melancholy night.
  I joy in dole; in languishment I pine.
My dearest friend is set; he was my sun,
With whom my mirth, my joy and all is done.

Yet if that age had frosted o'er his head,
  Or if his face had furrowed been with years,
I would not so bemoan that he is dead,
  I might have been more niggard of my tears.
But, O, the sun new-rose is gone to bed
And lilies in their spring-time hang their head.

Another of Gibbons's serious works is a setting of
the fine poem 'What is our life?' usually attributed to
Sir Walter Raleigh. This madrigal may be placed
amongst the very finest secular things ever written in
the polyphonic manner. It is characterized by a magni-
ficent dignity of style, and the part-writing is superb.
The varied moods suggested by the words are precisely
matched in the music, and this madrigal provides a
conspicuous instance of how the musician may add to
the glory of the poet's work; this point is especially
noticeable at such passages as 'Heaven the judicious
sharp Spectator is, That sits and marks still who doth
act amiss'; 'our graves that hide us', with the long
homophonic chords and the fall to the chord of E flat;
and again in the strong rhythmic measures at the words
'thus march we playing'. If he had never written anything else this madrigal alone would have qualified

Gibbons for a select place in the highest rank of the polyphonic composers.

Among other serious madrigals are settings of two stanzas from Spenser's *Faerie Queene*, and some lines beginning 'Now each flowery bank of May'. This latter contains some picturesque and suggestive music, but the meaning of the words is somewhat obscure; it works up to a fine climax at the end, but it is an extremely difficult madrigal to interpret satisfactorily.

'Dainty fine bird' and 'Ah dear heart' are exquisite examples of the typical madrigal, though both are far removed from all idea of gaiety; and on a more extended scale 'Fair is the rose' is also a splendid madrigal characterized by beautiful part-writing.

The leading feature of Gibbons's work is the independence of his part-writing. He rarely introduced a homophonic phrase, and in this matter his writing differs from that of almost all the other English madrigalists, including Byrd, whom he most nearly resembles in style. Noticeable examples, however, of the use of homophonic phrases occur in the latter part of Gibbons's 'Faerie Queene' madrigal. With reference to this detail a comparison of Gibbons's service in F with Byrd's short service is very illuminating. The musical phrases in Gibbons's work being somewhat more extended than was usual in the other composers, he was, as it were, weaving longer threads together, with the result that joints between the verbal phrases are more completely hidden in the closely woven texture. Gibbons resembles Byrd too in the austerity of his choice of subjects for his madrigals; like Byrd he also wrote no ballets or *fa las*, and, indeed, nothing in so light a vein even as Byrd's 'I thought that Love had been a boy' and a few others of that character; yet there is a quaint touch of humour in 'O that the learned poets', and especially in the ingenious academic passage with which that madrigal opens.

It has been said in connexion with his Church music that Gibbons, standing at the cross-ways, looked both backward and forward; back to Byrd and Tallis, forward to Blow and Purcell. As a madrigal writer he looked backward but not forward; and, viewing his work after a lapse of three hundred years, we can count this a fortunate circumstance, for although Gibbons looked back for his model and style, he expressed himself with such intense beauty and depth of meaning in that style that, in a sense, he put the final coping-stone on the achievements of the secular polyphonists. He stands in the select band of English madrigalists with Byrd, Wilbye, Weelkes, Morley, Ward, and Tomkins, and unquestionably his contribution to the general output of that great group, though small, was of a very individual nature and of a special type not found in the work of any of his contemporaries. Of Gibbons more than of any of the other English madrigalists it is true that his composership can be identified by the individuality of his style.

One other important piece of secular vocal music by Gibbons is a setting of the 'cries of London'. Weelkes, Dering, and Gibbons each wrote somewhat lengthy pieces of music incorporating and stringing together a large number of the 'cries' of London, associating them with their traditional musical phrases; the voices are accompanied by viols. It is an error to suppose that the actual music of the cries was composed in the sense of being originated by these musicians. Among the manuscripts in which these three compositions are found there are also two more sets of 'cries' to which no name is attached. One of these follows Weelkes's 'cry' in B.M. Add. MSS. 18936–9, and the other follows Gibbons's 'crye' in B.M. Add. MSS. 17792–6. This latter is called in some of the part-books 'The second London crie', and in others 'The laste of the London cryes'. There is no reason at all to suppose it is written by Gibbons. Dering also compiled a set of 'Country cries'.

Gibbons's 'London cry' is found complete in three different sets of manuscript part-books in the British Museum,[1] and there is also a single tenor part.[2] One of these sets of part-books is in the hand of Thomas Myriell[3] and is dated 1616, nine years before the

---

[1] B.M. Add. MSS. 17792–6; 29372–6; and 37402–6.
[2] B.M. Add. MS. 29427. [3] B.M. Add. MSS. 29372–6.

composer's death. Gibbons's composition is similar in design to the form of composition known as *In nomine*, the usual plain-song melody *Gloria tibi Trinitas* being assigned to one of the viols. It is a lengthy work, in two sections or parts. It opens with the watchman's call 'God give you good morrow, my masters, past three o'clock in a fair morning'. Then follows 'New mussels, new lilywhite mussels' and a great variety of 'cries', hawking various wares. The traditional melody of many of these has been preserved nowhere else. After the cry of 'new Wall-flete oysters' the town-crier breaks in to advertise in humorous terms the loss of a grey mare ' . . . lost this thirtieth day of February'. Among other cries introduced by Gibbons 'Poor naked Bedlam Tom's a-cold' is interesting in reference to *King Lear*, Act I, sc. ii: 'my cue is villanous melancholy with a sigh like Tom o' Bedlam,' and Act IV, sc. i: '*Glouc.* Sirrah, naked fellow,—*Edgar.* Poor Tom's a-cold!' The first section ends with 'So we make an end' in which phrase all four voices join. The second section opens with 'A good sausage, a good, an' it be roasted', and after a great variety of cries it ends with 'Twelve o'clock! look well to your lock, your fire and your light; and so, good night!'

No solo songs by Gibbons are known to the present writer. Sir Frederick Bridge[1] mentions 'A soldier's farewell to his mistress', beginning 'My love adieu',

---

[1] *Twelve Good Musicians*, by J. F. Bridge, p. 37.

but he gives no reference to the source and the song is not in the catalogues of any of the leading libraries.

List of Secular Vocal Music by Orlando Gibbons

The First Set of Madrigals and Mottets of 5. Parts: apt for Viols and Voyces Newly composed by Orlando Gibbons Batcheler of Musicke, and Organist of his Maiesties Honourable Chappell in Ordinarie. London: Printed by Thomas Snodham the Assigne of W. Barley 1612.

Contents

1. The silver swan.
2. O that the learned poets.
3. I weigh not Fortune's frown (*part* i).
4. I tremble not at noise of war (*part* ii).
5. I see Ambition never pleased (*part* iii).
6. I feign not friendship (*part* iv).
7. How art thou thralled! (*part* i).
8. Farewell, all joys (*part* ii).
9. Dainty fine bird.
10. Fair ladies, that to love (*part* i).
11. 'Mongst thousands good (*part* ii).
12. Now each flowery bank of May.
13. Lais, now old.
14. What is our life?
15. Ah, dear heart.
16. Fair is the rose.
17. Nay let me weep (*part* i).
18. Ne'er let the sun (*part* ii).
19. Yet if that age (*part* iii).
20. Trust not too much, fair youth.

A Crye of London (B.M. Add. MSS. 17792–6, 29372–6, 29427, 37402–6. Ch. Ch., Oxf., MS. 67, short score without words):

God give you good morrow (*part* i).
A good sausage (*part* ii).

CHAPTER V

Instrumental Music

INSTRUMENTAL music seems to have become
widely popular in England during the early years of the
seventeenth century. That a good deal of keyboard
music was written by the later Elizabethans has been a
matter of common knowledge for many years. As long
ago as the year 1847 a reprint of *Parthenia*, first published
in 1611, was issued to members of the Musical Antiquarian Society; it is true that it was full of careless
errors of transcription and was further marred by faulty
methods of editing, Gibbons's fine fantasia being especially ill-treated at Rimbault's hands in this reprint.
Nevertheless it served to bring the early English keyboard works of Byrd, Bull, and Gibbons to the notice
of modern musicians. More recently the whole of the
famous FitzWilliam Virginal Book was published in
modern notation under the editorship of Fuller Maitland and Barclay Squire, and this drew general attention to the fact that a very large quantity of keyboard
music was written in the reigns of Elizabeth and James
I, and that much of it was of considerable excellence.
Much has still to be done in reprinting the other

Virginal books of the period before the full extent of this music can be known and its value rightly appraised.

Few musicians, however, seem to be aware that a large amount of music was written for strings at this same period, although it has been generally understood that string instruments were in common use at the close of Elizabeth's reign, and that part of the equipment of a well-ordered house was a 'chest of viols'. A 'chest' consisted of a set of six viols, a sestet being then the normal standard for the 'consort', just as at a later date it was a string quartet. Musicians have supposed that the technique of string-writing at this date differed little, if at all, from that of vocal part-writing; and considerable colour has been lent to this view for the reason that madrigals were so generally described as being 'apt for viols or voices'; in other words, madrigals could either be sung in the ordinary way or else treated as songs without words and played on viols. It was Weelkes who first employed the phrase 'apt for voices or viols' in 1600. It is true that the madrigals are somewhat unsatisfactory to play on strings for the reason that the technique is necessarily a vocal one, especially in reference to the reiteration of the notes, and it does not appeal to the ordinary string-player. But very soon after 1600 the composers began to develop a definite and independent instrumental technique; that this was so is less apparent at first sight, because of the length of the notes in which they habitually expressed themselves, according to the convention of their day; for when music is written in terms of a minim unit rather than that of a crotchet, the eye of a modern string-player does not so readily recognize the phrases and groups of notes as he does when the same phrases are expressed in terms of crotchets and quavers. An excellent example of this may be seen in the triple rhythm section of Byrd's six-part Fantasia in his 1611 set. As printed with the original note-values in the present writer's English Madrigal School[1] it does not appeal to the string-player's eye, yet the same passage looks as clear as any similar phrase in Haydn or Mozart when set out and printed in notes of half the value.[2] And this principle applies to all the instrumental compositions of that date.

Gibbons wrote more string music than most of his contemporaries,[3] and the style is in marked contrast to his purely vocal work. There are altogether as many as thirty-seven known compositions for strings by him surviving to-day. As many as twenty-four fantasies for string trio are known, besides a Galliard for trio. Nine of these were published in Gibbons's lifetime under the

---

[1] Vol. xvi, p. 172.

[2] Byrd's Fantasia (No. 1) for string sestet, ed. E. H. Fellowes. Stainer and Bell; and Byrd, Complete Works. Vol. xvii (1950). Stainer and Bell.

[3] The extent of Gibbons's work in this department was unknown to the present writer two years ago when he omitted his name among those who with Byrd were the pioneers of chamber-music for strings at this period in his book on William Byrd, p. 102. [Clarendon Press, 1923].

title: 'Fantasies of Three parts Composed by Orlando
Gibbons Batchelour of Musick and Late Organist of his
Maiesties Chappell Royall in ordinary. Cut in Copper,
the like not heretofore extant. London: At the Bell in
S^t. Paul's Church Yard.' The work was dedicated, with
a very brief address, 'To the pattern of virtue and my
honorable friend Mr. Edward Wray, one of the Groomes
of his Maiesties bed Chamber.' The exact date of publi-
cation is not known, for there is no record of the work
in the registers at the Stationers' Hall. As a novelty,
'cut in copper', it would seem to have been published
before *Parthenia* and therefore about 1610. The expression 'Late Organist' cannot be explained, for Gibbons
held his post without interruption from 1603 until his
death. These fantasies become far more intelligible
when set out in notes of shorter value,[1] but a special
feature of them is the freedom and independence of the
rhythmic treatment; good examples of this freedom are
to be found in the concluding passage of No. 3, and in
the opening of No. 8; in this latter instance a triple
phrase, made up of a dotted quaver and three semi-
quavers, runs in sequence right across the normal bar-
periods and with complete independence in each string
part. It is partly because the free rhythms have not
always been recognized that these nine fantasies have
been misunderstood and regarded as immature. When

---

[1] *Nine Fantasies of Three Parts* by Orlando Gibbons, ed. by E. H. Fellowes.
Stainer and Bell.

properly interpreted they are no more alike each other than any two of Bach's works. Most of them are written in fugal style, but Nos. 6 and 7 are exceptions. No. 6 is especially charming, and the recapitulation of the opening phrase in the coda is very beautiful, as well as interesting in relation to the history of Form. Manuscript text of these nine fantasies is to be found in the British Museum, the Bodleian, and Christ Church libraries.

For performance the first four are suitable for violin, viola, and violoncello, and the remaining five for two violins and violoncello. Fifteen more fantasies by Gibbons for string trio are in manuscript in Archbishop Marsh's library in Dublin. These are all in score, but Nos. 9 and 12 of them are also included in separate partbooks in the same library, together with a short Galliard of three parts. Nos. 9–12 of this set are in early partbooks at Christ Church, Oxford. The Marsh set are very similar in style to the nine that were printed in Gibbons's time. As in the printed set, the combination of instruments is varied; in Nos. 9, 13, 14, and 15 the compass requires that a violin and two 'cellos should be employed in performance. Nos. 10, 11, and 12 are especially attractive, and these may be played with violin, viola, and 'cello.

For string quartet there are two fantasies in the Christ Church library. Both these pieces are written with two instruments of low compass at the bottom, and this is the meaning of the expression 'for double base' in the manuscript, implying two bass instruments, not a 'double-bass' in the modern orchestral sense; but these fantasies are very effective when transposed up for the ordinary combination of two violins, viola, and violoncello.[1] As in the three-part fantasies, there is much freedom of rhythmic treatment in certain passages, but these quartets are among the most attractive instrumental works of the period. An *In nomine* of four parts is in the Bodleian Library.

For quintet there are three *In nomines*. One of these appears to have been especially popular, for manuscript text of it is to be found in four different libraries: namely, the Bodleian, Christ Church, St. Michael's, Tenbury, and Marsh; it contains some very florid passages. No. 2 is also in the three first-named libraries. Both these compositions are more interesting than most *In nomines*. The third five-part *In nomine* is found only in the Bodleian Library. A five-part Pavan in the British Museum, entitled 'Deleroy Pavan', is incomplete; only three of the five parts are known.

For six strings there are four fantasies in the Christ Church library. Of these No. 1 is incomplete, and the most interesting is No. 3, which begins with a very characteristic little figure treated imitatively in all the parts. No. 4 opens, in contrast to the ordinary fugal style, with the four lower instruments playing

---

[1] *Two Fantasies for string quartet* (Score and Parts), ed. by E. H. Fellowes. Stainer and Bell.

together; it is in slower measure than the other fantasies and corresponds more nearly to the slow movement of the eighteenth and nineteenth centuries. The Pavan and Galliard for six strings is a delightful work;[1] manuscript text of it is to be found in Marsh's library and also in the Bodleian Library. It follows the straightforward pattern and rhythm of those popular dance forms.

Turning to keyboard works, it must be stated again that Orlando Gibbons was regarded as the greatest player of his day. This was indeed high praise when it is remembered that Byrd and Bull were among his contemporaries; for there can be no doubt that these two were certainly *virtuosi* of the highest order. Yet contemporary authority can be quoted to support the claim that Gibbons was the finest executant of this brilliant group of players. The letter of John Chamberlain to Sir Dudley Carleton, dated the 12th June 1625, has already been quoted, in which he says that Gibbons had 'the best hand in England'. This very definite statement of his complete supremacy is supported by the passage from Hacket's *Scrinia reserata* already referred to on page 40, in which he said that in 1623 'the organ (in Westminster Abbey) was touch'd by the best finger of that Age Mr. Orlando Gibbons'. The compositions of a brilliant executant have always a special interest.

---

[1] *Pavan and Galliard* by Orlando Gibbons, ed. by E. H. Fellowes (Score and Parts). Stainer and Bell.

In the case of Gibbons his austere personality and his profound musicianship guarded him from the obvious dangers that have so often beset the virtuoso-composers; he never lowered his art for the purposes of vulgar display.

The keyboard works of Gibbons are of far greater regularity of outline and rhythm than his compositions for strings; overlapping and irregular rhythms are comparatively rare, whereas in the vocal and string music they abound freely. The reason for this difference of character will be obvious when it is remembered that the difficulty of a single player controlling several different rhythms simultaneously must necessarily be far greater than when each separate part is controlled by individual performers, whether string-players or singers.

Gibbons co-operated with Byrd and Bull in a collection of the works of these three which was published in 1611 under the title of *Parthenia*. Gibbons was much the youngest of the three, and it is evidence of the high estimation in which both Byrd and Bull must have held him that he should have been invited to contribute to this famous collection. Gibbons in 1611 was only twenty-eight, whereas Byrd was sixty-eight and Bull nearly fifty.

The full title of the work was 'Parthenia or The Maydenhead of the first musicke that euer was printed for the Virginalls Composed by three famous Masters

William Byrd Dr. John Bull & Orlando Gibbons. Gentilmen of his Maties: most Illustrious Chappell. Ingrauen by William Hole. Lond: print: for M Dor: Euans. Cum priuilegio. Are to be sould by G. Lowe print^r in Loathberry'. It was dedicated to 'Prince Frederick Elector Palatine of the Reine: and his betrothed lady Elizabeth the only daughter of my Lord the King'. It contains the conventional number of twenty-one compositions, a number so often observed in the musical publications of this date. Of these Byrd contributed eight, Bull seven, and Gibbons six. Of Gibbons's six pieces much the most noteworthy is the 'Fantazia of Foure Parts' (No. 17). This is undoubtedly a great work. Writing in Grove's *Dictionary of Music and Musicians* (second edition), Fuller Maitland says of this Fantasia that it is 'so masterly in design, so finely invented and so splendidly carried out, that we meet with nothing at all comparable to it until the time of Bach'. It is unfortunate that Rimbault's edition of this fantasia in the reprint of *Parthenia*, published by the Musical Antiquarian Society, is such an inaccurate version of the original. Another of Gibbons's pieces which may be said to foreshadow Bach is the prelude with which *Parthenia* closes; some of the sequences towards the end of this prelude, though they became familiar formulae in the eighteenth century, were quite novelties in 1611. Gibbons's 'Queenes Command' and 'the Lord of Salisbury' Pavan are also in this same collection; the former is a set of variations upon a folk-song tune.

The famous FitzWilliam book is much the largest of the known virginal books of the period. It contains nearly three hundred pieces; but, strangely enough, Gibbons is almost entirely excluded from it. His name only appears once in the whole collection, and the piece is his *Parthenia* Pavan. His set of variations on the song known as 'The woode soe wilde' was also included, but without his name, and the text of it is incomplete, ending abruptly after a single bar of the fifth section. Complete text of this composition has fortunately survived elsewhere.[1] Seeing that Gibbons was generally held to be the finest executant of his day, it would almost seem as if his work had been deliberately excluded for some personal reason by the compiler of the FitzWilliam book, which was put together apparently about the year 1621 or 1622.

A coranto, described elsewhere as a Toye with variations, is the only other composition by Gibbons in the FitzWilliam book. It is No. 203 in the book, but it is given anonymously. This coranto is definitely assigned to Gibbons in Benjamin Cosyn's virginal book, and also in the virginal book now in the Drexel collection in the New York Public Library. Much valuable research work has recently been carried out by Miss Margaret H. Glyn in connexion with the virginal music of the

[1] B.M. Add. MS. 31403.

Elizabethan and Jacobean composers; the study of little-known collections, more particularly the Drexel book and the collections at Christ Church, Oxford, and the Paris Conservatoire of Music, has enabled her not only to discover several virginal pieces by Gibbons that were not otherwise known, but also to identify as his work many compositions which appeared anonymously in other collections and in some instances under the names of other composers. The list given at the conclusion of this chapter is compiled by kind permission of Miss Glyn from her book,[1] together with some further details communicated by her.

In this same book an interesting account is given as to how some of the compilers of the Jacobean virginal books had no scruple in altering and 'editing' the text according to their own fancy; and how also they would occasionally substitute a fresh composer's name for the true one. On this point Miss Glyn says:[2] 'Making all due allowance for careless mistakes and omissions, we find a good deal that cannot be anything but intentional perversion of texts and composers' names. . . . Three pieces by Cosyn, signed by him in his own autograph book . . . are in the FitzWilliam MS. given to Bull.' One of these is 'The King's Hunt', which, on the evidence of the FitzWilliam book alone, has unfortunately, and apparently quite erroneously, come to be regarded

---

[1] *About Elizabethan Virginal Music and its Composers*, M. H. Glyn. William Reeves. [2] Op. cit., p. 43.

without question as Bull's; the FitzWilliam text of this piece would appear, as regards many details, to be an inaccurate version of Cosyn's work as represented in his own autograph. It was clearly, says Miss Glyn, 'part of the business of the FitzWilliam compiler to *edit*, for one of Bull's own pieces is altered almost past recognition, and this is also the case with a Toye and Variations by Gibbons, and a variation set "Pakington's Pounde" by Cosyn, all shortened, mutilated and inserted anonymously'.

Of the 'Queenes Command', already mentioned as being in *Parthenia*, another text, only the first twelve bars of which are the same as that of *Parthenia*, is found in Cosyn's virginal book formerly in the Royal Library at Buckingham Palace and now in the British Museum. This piece is assigned to Cosyn in the Index, but to Gibbons at the conclusion of the music. Miss Glyn has discovered that both the title and signature of this piece have been taken out with acid and that the name of Gibbons was subsequently inserted in Cosyn's hand, but that in a strong light Cosyn's name can still be discerned under that of Gibbons. On these facts the same author has built up a theory, for details of which, as for many other matters of interest concerning the virginal music of Gibbons and other composers, the reader is referred to her book.

List of Works for Strings by Orlando Gibbons

Of six parts

Four Fantasies. Ch. Ch., Oxf., MS. 21. (No. 1 is incomplete)

Pavan and Galliard. Marsh's Library, Dublin, MSS. Z. 3. Tab. 4. 1–6. Bodleian MSS. Mus. Sch. E. 437–42.

Of five parts

Three 'In nomines':

    No. 1. Bodleian MSS. Mus. Sch. D. 212–16. Ch. Ch., Oxf., MSS. 423–8. Tenbury MS. 302. Marsh's Library, Dublin, MSS. Z. 3. Tab. 4. 1–6.

    No. 2. Bodleian MSS. Mus. Sch. D. 212–16. Ch. Ch., Oxf., MSS. 423–8. Tenbury MS. 302.

    No. 3. Bodleian MSS. Mus. Sch. D. 212–16.

Pavan 'Deleroye', B.M. Add. MSS. 30826–8 (two parts wanting).

Of four parts

Two Fantasies. Ch. Ch., Oxf., MSS. 732–6.

'In nomine'. Bodleian MSS. Mus. Sch. D. 212–16.

Of three parts

Nine Fantasies. Printed *circa* 1610. In manuscript: B.M. Add. MSS. 34800 and 17792–6. Bodleian MSS. Mus. Sch. D. 245–7. Ch. Ch., Oxf., MSS. 401–2 (1st part wanting); 21 (om. No. 3), 61, 64, 66 (Nos. 1–6); 473–8 (Nos. 1–6), 459–62 (Nos. 1, 2, 5, 6). Nos. 5 and 8 are also in Bodleian MS. Mus. Sch. F. 575.

Fifteen Fantasies. Marsh's Library, Dublin, MSS. Z. 2. Tab. 1. 13.

    Nos. 9–12 are also in Ch. Ch., Oxf., MSS. 732–5.

    Nos. 9 and 12 are also in Marsh's Library, Dublin, MSS. Z. 3. Tab. 4. 1–6.

Galliard. Marsh's Library, Dublin, MSS. Z. 3. Tab. 4. 1–6.

List of Keyboard Works by Orlando Gibbons

★ Found in this manuscript without composer's name.
★★ Found in this manuscript under the name of another composer.

Alman in D min. . .	N.Y. Drex. 5612, 122.
Alman in C . . .	Cosyn 63. N.Y. Drex. 5612.
Alman in G . . .	Cosyn 79.
Alman or Italian Ground .	B.M. Add. MS. 10337.★★ Add. 36661. Ch. Ch. 1113. N.Y. Drex. 5612. Paris 18548.
Alman or King's Juell .	B.M. Add. 36661. Cosyn (twice).
French Alman . . .	B.M. Add. 10337.★ Cosyn. N.Y. Drex. 5612.★
Ayre or Toy in A min. .	Ch. Ch. 1003. Ch. Ch. 1113. N.Y. Drex. 5612. Paris 18570. II.★
French Ayre . . .	B.M. Add. 36661.
Coranto in D min. . .	B.M. Add. 36661. Paris 18548.
Coranto in D min. . .	Paris 18548, 44.★★ N.Y. Drex. 5611.
Coranto in D min. . .	N.Y. Drex. 5611.
Coranto or Toy in A min.	B.M. Add. 23623★★ (called 'Adieu Coranto'). Cosyn. Fitz. 203.★ N.Y. Drex. 5612.
French Coranto . .	B.M. Add. 36661.
Galliard. Lady Hatton .	Cosyn. Ch. Ch. 1113. N.Y. Drex. 5612.★
Galliard. Lord of Salisbury	Parth. Ch. Ch. 431.★ N.Y. Drex. 3612.
Galliard in A min. . .	Cosyn 55.
Galliard in A min. . .	B.M. Add. 36661. Cosyn 58. N.Y. Drex. 5612.★★
Galliard in C . .	Parth. N.Y. Drex. 5612.★
Galliard in D min. . .	Cosyn 62.

Galliard in D min.	Cosyn 72.
Pavan, Lord of Salisbury	Parth. Fitz. 292. N.Y. Drex. 5612. Paris 18570. II.*
Pavan in D min.	B.M. Add. 29996. Cosyn. Paris 18548.
Pavan in G min.	N.Y. Drex. 5612.
Prelude in A min.	Cosyn. Ch. Ch. 47 (called Running Fantasia). N.Y. Drex. 5611.** Paris 18570. II.*
Prelude in G	Parth. B.M. Add. 22099. Add. 23623, 5.** Add. 23623, 44.** Add. 31403. Ch. Ch. 47. Ch. Ch. 89. N.Y. Drex. 5612. Paris 18570. I.

FANTASIES:

Fantasy in A min.	Cummings.
Fantasy in A min. (Plainsong)	Ch. Ch. 1113, 68.
Fantasy in A min.	Parth. B.M. Add. 31403, 20. Paris 18548.*
Fantasy in A min.	B.M. Add. 31403, 12. Cosyn 84. Ch. Ch. 1113, 66 and 1142 A.
Fantasy in A min.	B.M. Add. 31403, 18. Cosyn 18. Ch. Ch. 1113, 65.
Fantasy in C	B.M. Add. 31403, 16. Add. 36661. Cosyn 83.
Fantasy in C	B.M. Add. 31403, 14. Cosyn 82. Ch. Ch. 47 and 1176.
Fantasy in D min.	Cosyn 73. Cummings.
Fancy in D min.	B.M. Add. 31403, 19. Cosyn 60.
Fancy in D min.	B.M. Add. 36661, 4. Ch. Ch. 1142 A.
Fancy in D min.	Cosyn 77.
Fantasy in G min.	Cosyn 81.
Fantasy in G	Ch. Ch. 1113, 72.
Two Fancies in G (voluntaries)	Paris 18546.

Fantasy for Double Orgaine	Cosyn.
In Nomine. . . .	B.M. Add. 36661. Cosyn. Ch. Ch. 1113, 63.

MASKES:

The Fairest Nimphs . .	B.M. Add. 10337.* Add. 36661. Paris 18546.*
Lincolne's Inne Maske .	Paris 18548.
The Temple Maske . .	Cosyn. N.Y. Drex. 5612. Paris 18548.
Welcom Home . . .	Ch. Ch. 437. N.Y. Drex. 5612.* Paris 18548.*

VARIATIONS:

The Queenes Command .	Parth. Ch. Ch. 47. N.Y. Drex. 5611,** Drex. 5612.
Ground	N.Y. Drex. 5612.
Pescod Time (The Hunt's up)	Cosyn. N.Y. Drex. 5612.
Sarabrand . . .	Ch. Ch. 1175. N.Y. Drex. 5611.
Whoope do me no harm .	Ch. Ch. 47 and 431. Paris 18570, II.*
The Woode soe wilde .	B.M. Add. 31403. Add. 36661. Fitz. 40.*

The sources quoted in this list are: *Parthenia*; and the following manuscripts: British Museum Additional MSS. 10337, 22099, 23623, 29996, 31403, 36661; Benjamin Cosyn's MS., now at the British Museum, formerly at Buckingham Palace; Christ Church, Oxford, MSS. 47, 89, 431, 1003, 1113, 1142A, 1175, 1176. The FitzWilliam Virginal Book, FitzWilliam Museum, Cambridge. A manuscript formerly in the possession of Dr. W. H. Cummings. Manuscripts 5611 and 5612 in the Drexel Collection in the New York Public Library. Paris Conservatoire of Music, MSS. 18546, 18547 (in the hand of Thomas Tomkins), 18548 (in the hand of Cosyn) and 18570, i and ii.

APPENDIXES

APPENDIX I

Grant of Letters of Administration of the Property of Orlando Gibbons to his Widow

Wills of the Dean and Chapter of Westminster, 1626, A. III. 104

Adō Orlandi Gibbons—decimo tertio die mensis Julii anno dñi 1626 emāt [emanavit] commissio concessa Elizabethe Gibbons relče [relictae] Orlandi Gibbons nūp [nuper] civitatis Westm̄ gēn [generosi] defuncti ad addmñ [administrandum] bona dči [dicti] defuncti prius de bene &c ac de ex̄do [exhibendo] Inⁱʲ [Inventarii] et reddendo comm̄ &c iurat.

APPENDIX II

Nuncupative Will of William Gibbons

Camb. Arch. Court, vol. v, fo. 183 (now at Peterborough)

In the name of God Amen in the moneth of October in the yeare of our Lord God 1595 Willm̄ Gibbon of Cambridge in the Countie of Cambridge musitian being sicke in body but of a good & perfect minde and memorie made and declared his last Will and testam̄ nūcupative in manner and forme following viz First he gave & cōmended his soule to almightye god and his bodye he comended to xρstian buriall And as touchinge his worldlie goodes

wherew^th god had blessed him he disposed as followeth viz. he willed that Marie Gibbon his Wife should have all his goods whatsoev̂ to dispose amongest his children as she should thinck convenient and at her discretion Witnesses whereof
Humfrye Tredwaye M^r of Arts and Edward Gibbons Batchelour of Musicke

Prov. 13 Nov. 1595 by Marie Gibbon the relict.

APPENDIX III

Will of Mary Gibbons, Widow

Camb. Arch. Court, vol. vi, fo. 152 (now at Peterborough)

IN nomine dei Amen the seaventeenth daye of March in the year of o^ur Lord God 1602. I Mary Gybbons of Cambridge in the Countie of Cambridge Wydowe though Sicke in body yet whole in mynde and memory doe institute & ordeyne this my last Will and Testament in manner and forme following first I bequeath my soul to god who gave yt me assuredlie beleeving & trusting in Jesus Christ and in him only to be saved And my body to the earth from whence it came to lye as neere my deceased husband as convenientlye I maye Itm I give & bequeath to the poore of Trinitye parishe in Cambridge twentie shillings Itm̄ I give & bequeath to Elizabeth Dyer my daughter Sixe and twentie pounds thirteene shillings and fower pence of good and lawful money of England to be paied her within two moneths next after my death Itm I give unto Jane Gibbons my daughter twenty six pounds thirteene shillings fower pence of lawful English money to be paied her within one yeare next after my death I give more unto my Said daughter Jane Gibbons a mourninge gowne yf she be present at my funerall Itm I give to Ferdinando Gibbons my Sone twenty six pounds thirteene shillings fower pence to be paied him when he shallbe 23 years of age Itm I give to Orlandoe

Gibbons my Sonne twenty six pounds thirteen shillings fower
pence to be paied him when he shallbe one & twenty yeares of
age Itm I freelie acquitt Thomasin Hopper my daughter of that
Six pounds for wch. her husband standeth endebted unto me
reserveinge to my Executor the xx^s wch he hath in his hands the
debt amounting (as I take it) to vii^{li} x^s Itm I give my Sonne
Edward Gibbons & his wief each of them a mourning gowne
Item I give my Sonne Dyer & his wief each of them a mourning
gowne Itm I give my two Sonnes Ferdenando and Orlando each
of them a mourning cloake Itm I give my Sonne in Lawe Xpofer.
Edmondes a mourning cloake and his wief Marye a mourning
gowne Itm I give my daughter Joane Gibbons the wief of my
Sonne Ellis Gibbons a mourning gowne Alwaies provided yf they
be p̄sent at my buryall Itm I give to Mary Gibbons the daughter
of my Sonne Edward a peece of Silver plate to the full value of
five pounds and to his daughter Joane a peece of Silver plate to
the value of fortie Shillings to be paied them and either of them
within one yeare next after my death Itm I give Elizabeth Gibbons my niece five pounds of lawful English money when she
shallbe sixe and twentie yeares of age Itm I give to Mr Tredway
a ringe of twentie shillinges price within two moneths after my
death Itm I give and bequeath to my Sone Ellis Gibbons all the
rest of my goods & chattells whatsoever moveable or unmoveable
my debtes and funeralls first discharged whom (being fullie resolved of his zeale to god and dutifull affection to me) I make full
& sole Executor of this my last Will and Testament In witness
whereof I have set my hand and seale to these p̄sents the daye and
yeare above written in the yeare of her Ma^{ts} Reigne 45 The
marke of Mary Gibbons.

Sealed & subscribed in the p̄sence of
     James Deyer   Orlando Gibbons

After the making of this my last Will and Testament I thought

yt convenient upon speciall causes me thereunto moveing to bestowe more upon my daughter Hopper my best gowne and silck apron And whereas I bequeathed unto Mary Gibbons and Joane Gibbons the daughters of my Sonne Edward two peeces of plate I ordeyne that my Silver beaker shallbe for one for the eldest and the little guilte cupp for the younger wch were my estate greater should have bene more value And in regard that my Sonne Ferdenando standeth endebted unto me in the summe of Tenn pounds my Will ys yt should be deducted owt of his former portion And to this being in perfect Memory I subscribe the xith of April 1603 The marke of
  Marye Gibbons

Prov. 21 April 1603.

APPENDIX IV

Will of John Patten

P.C.C. 91 Swann

THE five and twentie daie of Februarye anno dñi 1622 And the twentieth yeare of the raigne of our Soveraigne Lord James . . . I John Patten of Westminster gent being sometimes visited with ,sicknes movinge me to feare sudden death doe therefore nowe beinge in perfect health and memorie thankes be to God make and ordaine this my last will and testament In manner and form followinge . . . I bequeath unto the children of Orlando Gibbons and my daughter his wife the sum of twoe hundreth poundes of lawfull money of England Item I give unto my sonne Richard Patten one hundreth and fiftie poundes to be paid him within five months after my decease Item I give unto Olyver Patten the sonne of Rich: Patten one hundreth pounds Item I give unto Sir William Walter and Henry Plumpton to each of them Fortie shillings apeece to make either of them a ring making them two

Overseers of this my last will and testament Item I give unto my godsonnes John Flower Henrie Plumpton and Robert Lane Fortie shillings apeece Item I give unto Rich: Goulding my man five pounds Item I give to the Children of Christs Hospital fiftie shillings And to the poore where I am buried fiftie shillings All the rest of my goodes houshould stuffe plate debts readie money and things whatsoever not given by this my will I give and bequeath unto Orlando Gibbons my sonne in lawe whom I make the sole executor of this my last will and testament Had made declared and given under my hand and state the daie and yeare above written in the presence of us whose names are subscribed John Patten Cromwell Walter Richard Gouldinge Peregrin Tomkins Thomas Garnett

Proved Sept 17th 1623 by Orlando Gibbons.

APPENDIX V

Will of Ellis Gibbons

P.C.C. 32 Bolein

In dei nomine amen I Ellis Gibbons weake in bodie but whole in minde do give and bequeath my sowle to the protection of the Almightie and my bodie to be buried as it shall please my executor Item I give unto my welbeloved wife my fee simple in Cambridge duringe her life And the lease in Pawles church yard during her life and after to come to my executor Item I give unto my brother Diers childe twentie poundes Item I give my brother Ferdinando twentie poundes Item I give my brother Orlando Twentie poundes Item I give and bequeath all my other goodes and chattells to my brother Edward Gibbons of Acton whom I make my full executor In witnes whereof I have hereunto sett my hand this fowretenth of Maie one thowsand six hundred and three.

APPENDIX V

By me Ellis Gibbons In the pr̄ce of us Jane Fleetewood Theophila Parsons James Diar and Elizabeth Dier

Proved May 18th 1603 by Edward Gibbons.

APPENDIX VI

Extracts from the Will of Elizabeth, Widow of Christopher Gibbons

P.C.C. 4 Drax

I ELIZABETH GIBBONS of the City of Westminster Widow Relict and Executrix of the last will and testament nuncupative of my late husband Christopher Gibbons late of Westm̄ aforesaid doctor of Musick and one of his Māties Musitians in ordinary deceased . . . my body . . . be devoutly buryed as neare my late husband as may be . . . Copiehold Messuage & Tenement and Lands . . . in Freesolke in the County of Southton which I now hold for the terme of my naturall life . . . to my daughter Elizabeth . . . £279. 10^s or thereabouts arrears of my said husband's salarie remaining yet unpaid in the Office of his Māties Treasury Chamber . . . my cousin Henry Sherborne of Bedfont . . . my daughter Anne . . . my daughter Mary if she shall ever hereafter return unto England . . . my sister Anne Ball . . . my brother Leonard Ball . . . my late husband's godson and my nephew Orlando Ball

dated March 19th 1677/8 proved Jan 22nd 1682/3

109

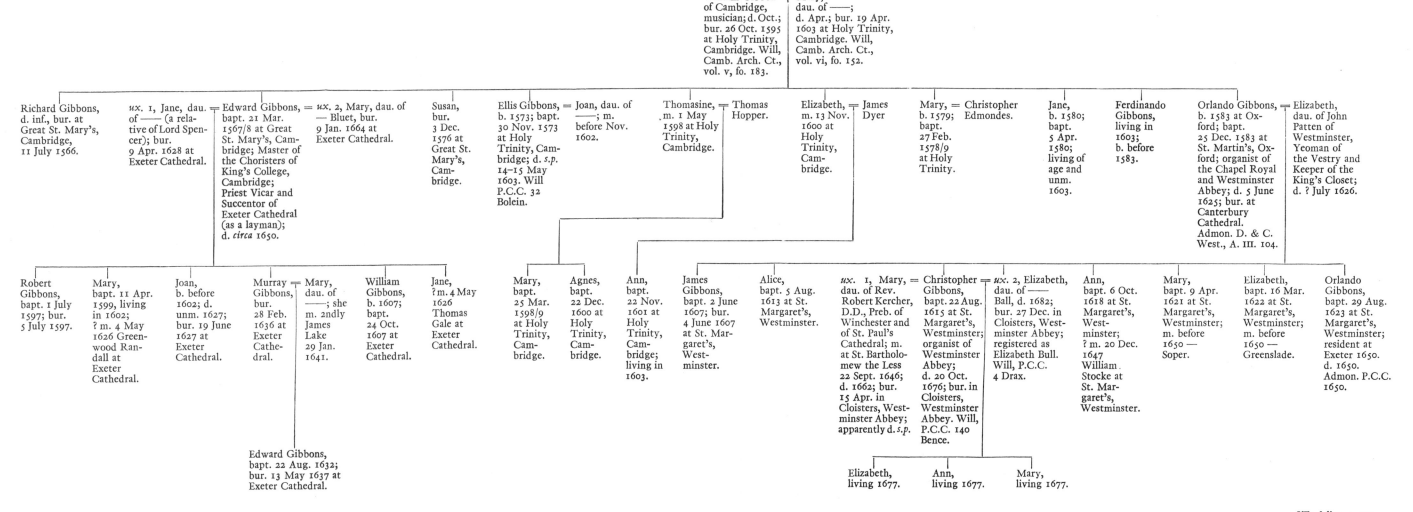

William Gibbons = Mary,
of Cambridge, │ dau. of ——;
musician; d. Oct.; │ d. Apr.; bur. 19 Apr.
bur. 26 Oct. 1595 │ 1603 at Holy Trinity,
at Holy Trinity, │ Cambridge. Will,
Cambridge. Will, │ Camb. Arch. Ct.,
Camb. Arch. Ct., │ vol. vi, fo. 152.
vol. v, fo. 183.

Richard Gibbons, | ux. 1, Jane, dau. = Edward Gibbons, = ux. 2, Mary, dau. of | Susan, | Ellis Gibbons, = Joan, dau. of | Thomasine, = Thomas | Elizabeth, = James | Mary, = Christopher | Jane, | Ferdinando | Orlando Gibbons, = Elizabeth,
d. inf., bur. at | of —— (a rela- | bapt. 21 Mar. | — Bluet, bur. | bur. | b. 1573; bapt. | ——; m. | m. 1 May | Hopper. | m. 13 Nov. | Dyer | b. 1579; | Edmondes. | b. 1580; | Gibbons, | b. 1583 at Ox- | dau. of John
Great St. Mary's, | tive of Lord Spen- | 1567/8 at Great | 9 Jan. 1664 at | 3 Dec. | 30 Nov. 1573 | before Nov. | 1598 at Holy | 1600 at | bapt. | bapt. | living in | ford; bapt. | Patten of
Cambridge, | cer); bur. | St. Mary's, Cam- | Exeter Cathedral. | 1576 at | at Holy | 1602. | Trinity, | Holy | 27 Feb. | 5 Apr. | 1603; | 25 Dec. 1583 at | Westminster,
11 July 1566. | 9 Apr. 1628 at | bridge; Master of | | Great St. | Trinity, Cam- | | Cambridge. | Trinity, | 1578/9 | 1580; | b. before | St. Martin's, Ox- | Yeoman of
| Exeter Cathedral. | the Choristers of | | Mary's, | bridge; d. s.p. | | | Cam- | at Holy | living of | 1583. | ford; organist of | the Vestry and
| | King's College, | | Cam- | 14–15 May | | | bridge. | Trinity. | age and | | the Chapel Royal | Keeper of the
| | Cambridge; | | bridge. | 1603. Will | | | | | unm. | | and Westminster | King's Closet;
| | Priest Vicar and | | | P.C.C. 32 | | | | | 1603. | | Abbey; d. 5 June | d. ? July 1626.
| | Succentor of | | | Bolein. | | | | | | | 1625; bur. at
| | Exeter Cathedral | | | | | | | | | | Canterbury
| | (as a layman); | | | | | | | | | | Cathedral.
| | d. circa 1650. | | | | | | | | | | Admon. D. & C.
| | | | | | | | | | | | West., A. III. 104.

Robert | Mary, | Joan, | Murray = Mary, | William | Jane, | Mary, | Agnes, | Ann, | James | Alice, | ux. 1, Mary, = Christopher = ux. 2, Elizabeth, | Ann, | Mary, | Elizabeth, | Orlando
Gibbons, | bapt. 11 Apr. | b. before | Gibbons, | dau. of | Gibbons, | ? m. 4 May | bapt. | bapt. | bapt. | Gibbons, | bapt. 5 Aug. | dau. of Rev. | Gibbons, | dau. of —— | bapt. 6 Oct. | bapt. 9 Apr. | bapt. 16 Mar. | Gibbons,
bapt. 1 July | 1599, living | 1602; d. | bur. | ——; she | b. 1607; | 1626 | 25 Mar. | 22 Dec. | 22 Nov. | bapt. 2 June | 1613 at St. | Robert Kercher, | bapt. 22 Aug. | Ball, d. 1682; | 1618 at St. | 1621 at St. | 1622 at St. | bapt. 29 Aug.
1597; bur. | in 1602; | unm. 1627; | 28 Feb. | m. 2ndly | bapt. | Thomas | 1598/9 | 1600 at | 1601 at | 1607; bur. | Margaret's, | D.D., Preb. of | 1615 at St. | bur. 27 Dec. in | Margaret's, | Margaret's, | Margaret's, | 1623 at St.
5 July 1597. | ? m. 4 May | bur. 19 June | 1636 at | James | 24 Oct. | Gale at | at Holy | Holy | Holy | 4 June 1607 | Westminster. | Winchester and | Margaret's, | Cloisters, West- | West- | Westminster; | Westminster; | Margaret's,
| 1626 Green- | 1627 at | Exeter | Lake | 1607 at | Exeter | Trinity, | Trinity, | Trinity, | at St. Mar- | | of St. Paul's | Westminster; | minster Abbey; | minster; | m. before | m. before | Westminster;
| wood Ran- | Exeter | Cathe- | 29 Jan. | Exeter | Cathedral. | Cam- | Cam- | Cam- | garet's, West- | | Cathedral; m. | organist of | registered as | ? m. 20 Dec. | 1650 —— | 1650 —— | resident at
| dall at | Cathedral. | dral. | 1641. | Cathedral. | | bridge. | bridge. | bridge; | minster. | | at St. Bartholo- | Westminster | Elizabeth Bull. | 1647 | Soper. | Greenslade. | Exeter 1650.
| Exeter | | | | | | | | living in | | | mew the Less | Abbey; | Will, P.C.C. | William | | | d. 1650.
| Cathedral. | | | | | | | | 1603. | | | 22 Sept. 1646; | d. 20 Oct. | 4 Drax. | Stocke at | | | Admon. P.C.C.
| | | | | | | | | | | | d. 1662; bur. | 1676; bur. in | | St. Mar- | | | 1650.
											15 Apr. in	Cloisters,		garet's,		
											Cloisters, West-	Westminster		Westminster.		
											minster Abbey;	Abbey. Will,				
											apparently d. s.p.	P.C.C. 140				
												Bence.				

Edward Gibbons,
bapt. 22 Aug. 1632;
bur. 13 May 1637 at
Exeter Cathedral.

Elizabeth, | Ann, | Mary,
living 1677. | living 1677. | living 1677.

[To follow p. 109